enter the story

7 EXPERIENCES TO UNLOCK THE BIBLE FOR YOUR STUDENTS

michael novelli

ZONDERVAN®

ZONDERVAN.com/
AUTHORTRACKER
follow your favorite authors

 youth
specialties

ZONDERVAN

Enter the Story: 7 Experiences to Unlock the Bible for Your Students
Copyright © 2010 by Michael Novelli

YS Youth Specialties is a trademark of YOUTHWORKS!, INCORPORATED and is registered with the United Sates Patent and Trademark Office.

This title is also available as a Zondervan ebook.
Visit www.zondervan.com/ebooks.

Requests for information should be addressed to:

Zondervan, *Grand Rapids, Michigan 49530*

Library of Congress Cataloging-in-Publication Data

Novelli, Michael.
    Enter the story : seven experiences to unlock the Bible for your students / Michael Novelli.
        p. cm.
    ISBN 978-0-310-66927-2 (pbk.)
    1. Bible—Study and teaching. 2. Christian education of teenagers. 3.
Christian education—Activity programs. I. Title.
BS600.3.N68 2010
220.6'10712—dc22   2009044723

Interior design by Mark Novelli, IMAGO

Printed in the United States of America

10 11 12 13 14 15 • 24 23 22 21 20 19 18 17 16 15 14 13 12 11 10 9 8 7 6 5 4 3 2 1

ACKNOWLEDGMENTS

Thanks to my wife Michele and my kids Angelo and Abrielle for letting me take "writing days" when I'd rather be outside in the sun with them.

Thanks to Kelly Dolan and Mark Novelli for dreaming and creating with me.

Thanks to all who helped shape and support the Merge Experiences on which this book is based: Kelli DeGroat, Seth McCoy, Brandon Brown, Jen Howver, Jared Johnson, Doug Scott, Andy Lindquist, Phil Shields, Lisa Jarot, Michele Novelli, Tory Dolan, Amy Dolan, Craig Joseph, Toni Mills, Karmen Koehn, Vanessa Amundsen, Amanda McLaughlin, Aimee Novelli, Chris Stewart, Janelle Robertson, Becky Ozinga, and Amelia Rabelhoffer.

Thanks to Chris Folmsbee for believing me and giving me the freedom to create crazy things.

A big thank you to Jay Howver, Roni Meek, and the rest of my friends at Zondervan/Youth Specialties. Roni had to deal with me constantly pushing back the deadlines and causing her stress!

Thanks to those who've inspired and encouraged me to keep creating: Mark Matlock, Lilly Lewin, Jeff Frazier, Mark Miller, Jon Keller, Steve Argue, Dave Livermore, Scott and Chris Douglas, John Witte, and Don Perini.

CONTENTS

PART ONE
BEFORE YOU ENTER!

INTRODUCTION
(PLEASE READ THIS FIRST!)

WHAT'S IN THIS BOOK?

This book includes seven experiences to help you and the group you lead *enter* God's Story. Detailed instructions, supply lists, and handouts are included. All of the handouts plus additional resources are available on the accompanying CD.

Every experience takes you on a journey to explore some of the major milestones in the Bible, helping your group learn, interact with, and place themselves as a part of God's continuing Story.

HOW DO I USE THESE EXPERIENCES?

Each experience has multiple stations or stopping points for groups to learn, interact, or pray. Most of these stations are oriented around interaction, while some focus on solo learning. These stations offer a lot of flexibility and options for how you use each experience. For example:

- Do one experience during your regular **youth program** (two to two-and-a-half hours).

- Do several experiences in a **retreat setting.**

- Do one experience over several weeks—in other words, do **a station a week** in a Sunday school class.

- Do a weeklong intensive **camp** using all of the experiences.

- Insert **your idea** here_____.

Please make the experiences you find in this book your own. Omit parts, add parts—whatever you need to do to connect with your group. More ideas for how to use these experiences can be found in the chapter "How to Set Up the Seven Experiences." You can also contact me at michael@echothestory.com if you want some help brainstorming uses for your ministry context.

WHY I WROTE THIS BOOK

I developed this book as a practical resource to provide simple ideas to help you take a group on a journey into the Bible Story. My hope is that as you immerse yourselves in God's Story, you'll discover profound meaning for your lives.

I also hope this book inspires you to dream beyond its pages, sparking creativity as you plan your own environments to help people learn and engage in deeper ways.

WHERE DID THESE EXPERIENCES COME FROM?

After more than a decade in youth ministry, I felt as though I'd tried everything to help teenagers connect with the Bible—with limited success. My students most often described Bible study as confusing, boring, irrelevant or too much work.

Through a chance encounter with a missionary to Africa, I discovered a unique, ancient way to engage people with God's Word, and it's rooted in the Hebrew tradition: Chronological Bible Storying. It's a sequential telling of Bible stories followed by a time of creative retelling and in-depth dialogue.

Soon I began a "storying experiment," telling and discussing Bible stories with a group of high schoolers for nine months straight. That experience completely transformed my youth group (and me), as they were truly shaped by God's Story.

The more we dove into the Story, the deeper their insights and questions became. One of my teens described it this way: "For the first time I felt like I could relate to the characters in the story...I saw them as real, plausible, and many-sided. They became real people doing real things...It challenged me to listen to God and obey his calling...to live in God's will fully. I need to surrender everything to God."

Another teen said, "It made me realize I need to live for the Author. God has a story for my life that I'm excited to discover and want to share with others. This amazing story is what we've been waiting for our entire lives."

I'd discovered more than just a new curriculum or fad. It was a different way of learning that helped teenagers build a lasting theological foundation. It challenged them to discover who they are and why they're here—to find themselves in a greater Story. (You can learn more about this method and my experiences with it at www.echothestory.com and in my first book, *Shaped by the Story: Helping Students Encounter God in a New Way*.)

These experiences fueled my desire to help others center their ministries on God's Story and "experiment" with more effective methods that help teens learn.

When I was given the opportunity to develop a new weeklong intensive discipleship event for a youth ministry organization a few years ago, naturally I wanted God's Story to be the centerpiece. With a team of people, I explored how to design an event that immersed teenagers in biblical narrative. The result is a unique event called Merge.

As a starting point, Merge uses Bible Storying—creative storytelling, retelling, and dialogue—each morning to help youth learn about God's Story and discover connections and implications. Each afternoon, youth groups participate in a Group Experience—an imaginative, hands-on activity that helps adolescents dig deeper into God's Story and discover meaning for their lives. Art and media, learning stations, and interactive experiences propel teenagers toward creative responses to the stories each evening. My hope for Merge is that teenagers are transformed and *merge* their stories with God's, joining in God's mission of love and restoration. (To find out more about Merge, go to: www.mergeexperience.com)

The seven experiences described in this book were originally developed for the Merge Event. I've also used them for youth group meetings and retreats over the past several years. I have used them effectively with both youth and adult groups. More than a thousand adolescents have gone through some version of these experiences, helping me make them what they are today. A dozen friends and colleagues also contributed to shaping them.

Given the right guidance and environment, teenagers will surprise us with their insights, creativity, and dreams to change the world. I hope you'll experiment with me, empowering young lives to see themselves as part of something bigger—a new way of living under God's reign that can change everything! Together, let's enter the Story.

STEP INTO THE STORY

ENTERING IN VERSUS TAKING OUT

We live in a culture of evaluation. People working in the media, news, and entertainment industries make millions of dollars as professional critics. Entire television shows, magazines, and blogs are dedicated to evaluating what people wear on the red carpet on the night of the Academy Awards. We love to watch shows like *American Idol* and *Dancing with the Stars* because we get to cast our votes and be the judges from the comfort of our own living rooms. We nod in agreement or wince in disapproval as celebrity judges dissect the talent of burgeoning celebrities. We eat this stuff up!

I believe our culture of evaluation and critique somehow influences way more than our choices in entertainment. I believe Americans are a people of comparison. We define ourselves by how we measure up to others.

I spent the better portion of my school years comparing everything about myself to others—my style, clothes, looks, attitude, abilities—trying to find the middle of the road so I'd blend in. It's kind of sad to think about now, but I was adrift in a sea of evaluation. I wish I could say I'm now completely free of this, but I believe we'd all admit that a culture of comparison has tainted us. My hope is that as someone who's given myself to follow Christ, God's Spirit will break me from my patterns of comparison and replace them with rhythms of compassion and love.

I'm concerned that a culture of evaluation is also alive in our churches. Many of us sit in the pews and on comfy, padded seats each Sunday, taking in carefully crafted programs that are designed to challenge and inspire. Often the first question asked during the ride home is, *"So what did you think of the sermon?"* or *"What was going on with that special music?"* or *"What did they teach in Sunday school?"* These questions may be asked with good intentions, but they emit an aura of evaluation. Unfortunately, many of us have become critics from the pew—consumers of church who feel a right to a certain quality of product being delivered to us and to our children. This mindset projects further into how we come to the Bible.

Even those of us with professional Bible training have been taught to use one primary approach to the Bible—analytical. The tool we've been given is a magnifying glass, so we can dissect each chapter, verse, and word. We parse and dig for the meaning behind the meaning in the smallest increments. We've become scientists attempting to turn the beautiful, mysterious stories and poems that make up most of the Bible into actionable and practical steps for living. I'm not suggesting that we discard the magnifying glass—it's a good tool to use at times. For instance, I've found it insightful and fascinating to explore the meaning of biblical words in their original language. Words can give us windows into context and culture that help bring greater understanding. This takes careful examination that only the magnifying-glass approach provides. But if this is our *only* approach to the Bible, then we've made it (and it's made us) into something it was never intended to be. This manifests itself especially in the way we teach the Bible.

Author Colin Harbinson explains, "As the biblical story unfolds, it does so in stories and poetry. In fact, approximately seventy-five percent of scripture consists of narrative, fifteen percent is expressed in poetic forms and only ten percent is propositional and overtly instructional in nature. In our retelling of the same story, we have reversed this biblical pattern. Today an estimated ten percent of our communication is designed to capture the imagination of the listener, while ninety percent is purely instructive."[1]

Theologian Richard Jensen puts it this way: "Our literate tradition trained us to find the ideas in the Bible and shape them in logical ways for the preaching task. We have learned how to use Scripture as the source of ideas we wish to inculcate in the life of our people. There is another possibility. We can also fill their heads with people! We can tell biblical stories in such a way that the characters of the Bible come to live in the hearts and minds of our listeners! One of the ways in which Christ can be formed within us is the way of biblical characters living within our consciousness."[2]

But the much more widespread emphasis on analyzing the Bible and repackaging it in the form of ideas has contributed to a culture of Christians who stand apart from the Bible in evaluation—not necessarily looking for errors, but viewing it with a critical eye and lumping Scripture into the same category as self-help books. We scan it for nuggets of truth, points of meaning, parables for life, axioms for leadership, and models for ministry—and some of it's there and certainly helpful. But this approach still puts us in a place where we're standing outside the Bible's Story, disconnected from its context and straining to see its relevance for our lives.

Even worse, we lose sight of the Bible's bigger story of redemption and restoration, and we miss how we're a part of this sweeping narrative.

---

1   Colin Harbinson, "Restoring the Arts to the Church: The Role of Creativity in the Expression of Truth," *Lausanne World Pulse Magazine* (online), July 2006, edited from a chapter in *The Complete Evangelism Guidebook*, Scott Dawson ed. (Grand Rapids, Mich: Baker Books, 2006), http://www.lausanneworldpulse.com/themedarticles.php/409/07-2006 (accessed May 15, 2008).
2   Richard A. Jensen, *Thinking in Story: Preaching in a Post-literate Age* (Lima, Ohio: CSS Publishing, 1993), 9.

But what if we decided to enter into the Bible instead of always trying to take from it? What if we stepped inside of this story instead of pulling it apart?

The Bible story doesn't make a lot of sense when just looked at from the outside and in bits and pieces. We must enter into it in order to see it. How do we *enter* into God's Story? I have a couple of suggestions:

EMPOWER OUR IMAGINATIONS AND SENSES

"Imagination is more important than knowledge. Knowledge is limited. Imagination encircles the world." —ALBERT EINSTEIN[3]

We must let go of our tendencies to analyze and extrapolate from Scripture and give ourselves freedom to explore and learn in new ways. If we're always taking a posture of evaluating the Bible, it will constrict us.

I'm not suggesting we check our brains at the door. On the contrary, I'm suggesting we think more deeply—using our imaginations, intuition, and creativity—to make meaningful connections. Exploring the Bible through these channels will take us to new places that our rational and evaluative minds couldn't go on their own.

What I'm suggesting is that we use story and experiential learning as a gateway to enter God's Story. These approaches to learning are fueled by imagination and are the foundation of the experiences you'll find in this book.

Author and theologian C. S. Lewis writes, "For me, reason is the natural organ of truth; but imagination is the organ of meaning. Imagination, producing new metaphors or revivifying old, is not the cause of truth, but its condition."[4]

Sarah Arthur, in her book *The God-Hungry Imagination*, writes, "Imagination gives us the ability to find and make purposeful patterns and even plotlines: in other words, the ability to find and make meaning." She continues, "Imagination is how we put things together. It's how we make connections between thought and experience, word and image, self and other, seen and unseen."[5]

I believe that imagination fuels the transformation process. It's the key to processing the abstract and building faith. It gives context and moves us toward learning that's internalized

3   As quoted in "What Life Means to Einstein: An Interview by George Sylvester Viereck" in *The Saturday Evening Post* Vol. 202 (26 October 1929), p. 117.

4   C.S. Lewis, *Selected Literary Essays*, ed. Walter Hooper (Cambridge University Press, 1969).

5   Sara Arthur, *The God-Hungry Imagination: The Art of Storytelling for Postmodern Youth Ministry* (Nashville, Tenn: Upper Room Books, 2007), 49, 53.

and acted upon. It helps us weave an interior pattern that makes sense of life. And in order to create the best environments for transformation, we must take every opportunity to cultivate imagination in our ministries.

To enter into stories requires us to empower our imaginations and transport ourselves into a different time. Bible stories are embedded in an ancient culture that we must creatively move to understand in order to participate in the story. The Hebrew word for *remember* is *zah-khor*, and it's a word that means much more than just recalling something from the past; it suggests active engagement—*reliving and participating in again.* We're called to help others participate again in the ancient stories of our spiritual ancestors. It's there that we can find meaning and purpose for our lives.

EXPLORE THE BIBLE AS A NARRATIVE

We're called to live in a story that's still unfurling. The Bible story isn't just a story from the past; it's a living story, one of vibrancy and dimension. It's incarnational, entering our lives differently than other stories can. God calls us to enter this story, allowing it to shape and guide our lives.

When engaged as narrative, the Bible Story has a subtle way of getting into our heads and under our skin. At first it seems nonintrusive because it's a faraway story about a distant people. But then it begins to work on us—the messages beneath the surface emerge, and we're captivated by its story. We find ourselves inside that story, identifying and empathizing with the characters. It becomes part of our experience and identity—it's now our story.

This is called *implication*, which has a much different meaning from *application*. Many of us have been trained to first ask, "How does the Bible apply to me?" Yet, application literally means "to put on the surface." Thus, as with a Band-Aid or salve, we try to administer the Scriptures to our own situations.

To be implicated is to be bound with, wrapped up, and twisted together like the strands of a rope. The word implicate comes from the Latin word meaning "folded in." We become intertwined and folded in to God's Story, and it speaks to and informs us in regard to who we are, and why we're here.

So our question moves from "How do I apply this to my situation?" to "What does this mean for the way I live my life?" We begin to seek our role in the story, rather than try to figure out what to do with it.

Implication calls us toward something—to redefine what we know, to a new way of life lived with our community of faith. God's Story cultivates hope within us. We begin to envision how we can change our community, our world, and ourselves.

Eugene H. Peterson, translator of *The Message*, describes it this way:

> Stories are the most prominent biblical way of helping us see ourselves in "the God story," which always gets around to the story of God making and saving us. Stories, in contrast to abstract statements of truth, tease us into becoming participants in what is being said. We find ourselves involved in the action. We may start out as spectators or critics, but if the story is good (and the biblical stories are very good!), we find ourselves no longer just listening to but inhabiting the story."[6]

As we enter into God's Story through narrative, a whole new world is open to us. We begin to get a sense of God's entire interconnected story and discover how it intersects with our own stories. The narrative, in turn, clarifies our place in God's Story and helps us take the focus off ourselves and aim it toward God's desires for the world. It's what gives shape and context to our lives as we follow in the ways of Jesus. If we allow it to speak into, inform, and reorder our lives, it will guide us to discover our role in God's kingdom.

ENTER THE BIBLE THROUGH STORIES AND EXPERIENCES

My hope is that the seven experiences in this book will help your group begin a journey of entering into the story and interacting with it in tangible and imaginative ways. I'm not an expert on Hebrew culture, but I do believe these experiences will help you step into the world of the Bible as you think about what it was like, pray, discuss, wonder, reflect, and rest awhile. If we let the stories surround us, God will do powerful things in our lives.

6   Eugene H. Peterson, "Introduction to the Book of Jonah," *The Message Remix*, 2nd ed. (Colorado Springs: NavPress, 2006), 1352.

LEARN THROUGH EXPERIENCE

Right out of college I jumped into full-time youth ministry by leading a group of junior highers. Without knowing how to lead or where to begin, I did what most youth pastors do—I copied the youth ministry I'd attended in high school. I worked to become an engaging presenter-preacher and sprinkled in a few fun activities. In my mind, if I were good at teaching, the results were up to God and the young people. I didn't think much about the methods or even how the teenagers might learn best.

After years of using this approach, I greatly improved my skills of presenting the truth. I infused more creativity into my teaching by using lots of visuals, props, and stories. When I taught during youth group, I felt as though the teens were usually engaged and responsive just based on their body language. My expectation was that the better I became at teaching, the more impactful my teaching would be in the lives of adolescents who were open to learn and change.

Soon I was overseeing a large ministry of high schoolers and junior highers—and with a big ministry budget. I had several full-time staff members and interns churning out creative programming each week.

But I began to notice a couple things. First, only a few teens seemed to take ownership for their learning and faith, while the majority seemed to be dependent on pastors or parents to motivate them, feed them, and help them grow. Second, the young people rarely remembered anything I taught them—except for my stories. Months later, they could recount the funny stories I'd told; but within *minutes* of my talk's conclusion, they had no idea as to the main idea of my message.

Those observations prompted me to explore how I could involve teenagers in their own learning. I was concerned they weren't engaged in their faith in deep ways. And this was glaringly evident when many of my strongest teens returned from college disinterested in Christianity altogether. I wondered, *Why are so many of them drifting from their faith? Is this just a part of their adolescent journey...or am I not helping these teenagers realize and connect with an authentic faith?* I suspected both were true.

A visit to my wife's school and second-grade classroom was eye-opening. Right away, I noticed a significant focus on multiple learning modes. Classrooms were arranged with designated areas to accommodate learning through sight, sound, and touch. Every subject's curriculum was adapted to meet the needs of left- and right-brain processing, including tools for multisensory teaching. I thought, *This is different than when I was in school.* As my wife and I dialogued about this, she shared how there was strong research and proven educational theory behind the structure of their classrooms and curricula.

I immediately began researching and experimenting with new ways of teaching and learning. As I did so, it felt as though I was entering a whole new world—one left largely unexplored by the church. This path led me toward focusing on storytelling and experiential learning.

TYPES OF LEARNERS

Educators typically identify three types of learners: Visual, auditory, and physical. Most of us are predominantly one type. But, depending on the environment, we may adapt to other types.

VISUAL LEARNERS

- Process information by watching
- Identify images to relate to an experience
- Respond well to images, graphics, symbols, diagrams, key words, and demonstrations

AUDITORY LEARNERS

- Process information by hearing
- Identify sounds to relate to an experience
- Respond well to spoken words, discussion, music, and poems

PHYSICAL (KINESTHETIC) LEARNERS

- Process information by touch and movement
- Identify feelings to relate to an experience
- Respond well to written assignments, object lessons, field trips, and participation

Which type of learner are you? Educational research indicates the majority of people in the United States (and worldwide) are visual learners, some estimate as high as 70 percent. I'm definitely one of them—with some kinesthetic tendencies mixed in. When I look back at my youth group and educational experiences, I now understand why I never learned well from being "talked at." If I couldn't visualize what I was learning and get involved with it, I struggled.

More than that, if I don't have a visual reminder of the things I need to get done, I often forget to do them. Don't ask me to memorize anything, please. And don't give me a list of directions for how to get somewhere. I'll nervously look at it every two seconds to make sure I haven't missed a turn or forgotten the next street. (Maybe you've driven behind me as I slow down at every street corner to look at the signs.) But if you show me a map, I get it—I capture the image in my head. Even better, if you drive me there once, I'll never forget how to get there. Visual learners need certain cues.

Technology is also affecting the way we learn. Teenagers are accustomed to interacting with information in visual and physical ways. Through the Internet they can pull up facts, video, and images about most anything. Then they can reshape it, mix it up, and recreate it as their own. Teens don't just watch videos on YouTube anymore. They remake them as a creative response. Technology is contributing to our impatience with one-directional communication. **The new norm for adolescents is creating while they learn.**

ACTIVE LEARNING

We could easily look at these learner types and come up with ideas for how to make our talks more interactive—adding cool videos and pictures, props, and so on. While that's all good and helpful, I believe we must take a giant step further. In order to really engage others, we must give them opportunities to be *active learners*.

In their article titled "Seven Principles for Good Practice in Undergraduate Education," Arthur W. Chickering and Zelda F. Gamson write, "Learning is not a spectator sport. Students do not learn much just by sitting in classes listening to teachers, memorizing prepackaged assignments, and spitting out answers. They must talk about what they are learning, write about it, relate it to past experiences and apply it to their daily lives. They must make what they learn part of themselves."[7]

---

7   Arthur W. Chickering and Zelda F. Gamson, "Seven Principles for Good Practice in Undergraduate Education," *American Association for Higher Education Bulletin* (March 1987), http://www.aahea.org/bulletins/articles/sevenprinciples1987.htm.

What is "active learning"? Simply put, it involves people in the learning process so they're participating and doing, not just receiving information verbally and visually. This could include discussing, reading, praying, problem solving, journaling, drawing, and working on projects—anything that gets people engaged in the process beyond just listening.

Active learning can take many forms, including hands-on activities, discovery learning, inquiry learning, experiential learning, problem-based learning, cooperative learning, and other approaches. Active learning is both "minds on" and "hands on," as it focuses on being both cognitively and physically active.

The most significant part of active-learning approaches is that they require young people to use higher-order thinking skills, such as reflection, analysis, evaluation, synthesis, and application. Active learning gives teenagers the responsibility and guidance to discover and create. The benefit is that when students are empowered to create and discover on their own, often they'll embrace their learning in deeper ways. In a real sense, active learning helps students become the teachers. Not only are they teaching themselves as they integrate content, they're motivated to offer insight and share discoveries with their peers.

So are you saying that giving a sermon or message is bad? No...I believe that approach has a place. What I'm saying is that any communication that's one-directional and focused just on listening, such as preaching and giving a lecture, is passive. Passive learning methods can only hold a person's attention for so long. Without being involved in our learning, we tend to quickly disengage and become disinterested. For this reason, I believe that passive learning methods are far less effective and should be used sparingly.

SO WHY DO WE EMPHASIZE PASSIVE FORMS OF TEACHING?

We assume the better the teaching delivery, the more people will learn. I spent years developing my skills as a presenter. It got me better-paying jobs with bigger churches in ministry, but I didn't see more life change. Even if you give a great sermon, you aren't helping teens learn unless you provide varied opportunities for them to process and connect your message to their own lives.

We teach the way we've been taught. We rarely leave the safety of what we know—even if it's not really connecting with our audience—unless we realize a better way. Let me encourage you: *There's a whole new world of effective teaching—and I'm only scratching the surface.*

We unknowingly assume that everyone will learn the same way we do. I had a friend tell me recently, "You need to base your entire storytelling stuff on these seven principles. It really works." Not for me. I can't remember lists, and they seem too formulaic. I'm sure some people love them though. But it seems as though teens today are becoming less and less linear and sequential. They don't tend to think in terms of words and concepts as much as in terms of images and stories. I believe that teaching supported by steps and lists is becoming less helpful and accessible to future generations who are processing information in new ways.

We expect teenagers to adjust and adapt to our teaching styles. We may think, *These adolescents just need to dig in, get some discipline, concentrate, and work at learning. (Just like I had to do.)* Sometimes learning is a matter of giving more initiative and effort, but that doesn't mean we don't need to adapt. With some of my most apathetic teenagers, I discovered that if I tried different learning methods or invested more energy in encouraging and challenging them toward their potential, they immediately took more initiative for their learning. Instead of asking, "How can I improve as a teacher?" we should be asking, "How can I improve students' learning?"

We're paid to be the experts. It's scary for us to consider not being the keeper of the information and the person with all the answers. That's a role that many pastors secretly enjoy, and it makes us feel important. In a digital age, information is becoming ubiquitous, making experts less essential. Don't worry—your church still needs you! Your role and focus just needs to change in order to empower others as learners. You must take on the posture of a co-learner, guide, and facilitator and relinquish some of your role as an expert "source of all knowledge."

CREATE SACRED SPACE

If you'd like more ideas for experiential learning, check out the book *Sacred Space* by Dan Kimball and Lilly Lewin. It's packed with resources and ideas. I've co-led some workshops with Lilly, and she's one of the most creative minds you'll find in this area.

We believe we aren't creative enough to try new teaching methods. We're all born creative. Spend any amount of time with a three-year-old and you'll soon agree! But somewhere along the way, many of us get the notion that we aren't creative. I don't buy it. I believe that most creativity is rooted in the confidence to express yourself and explore your imaginative side. Creativity is a muscle that you must exercise—it's in you, so work it!

We believe it takes too much time to create experiences. Active and experiential learning isn't as simple as preaching. It may involve a bit more preparation and creativity, and it definitely requires you to depend on others for help. But there are lots of resources out there to borrow from that will cut down your planning time and give you great ideas.

A LEARNER-CENTERED FOCUS

As we begin to study the most effective methods of helping others learn, we discover that moving from teacher- or lecture-based to learner-based methods is imperative. Years of research have shown that motivation, learning, and success are enhanced when learner-centered principles and practices are in place. Throughout North America, educational institutions on all levels have transitioned to a learner-centered philosophy of teaching.

Maryellen Weimer, author of *Learner-Centered Teaching,* says that in order for teaching to more effectively promote learning, our thinking and practices need to change in five key areas:

1. The Balance of Power

The effectiveness of learner-centered methods depends on teachers being able to step aside and let adolescents take the lead. However, having been at the center for so long, we may find it tough to leave that spot, even briefly.

2. The Function of Content

The underlying philosophy is that young people learn best not only by receiving knowledge, but also by interpreting it, learning through discovery, and setting the pace for their own learning.

SOME KEYS TO LEARNER-CENTERED TEACHING

1. Assume that young people are capable learners who will blossom as power shifts to a more egalitarian classroom.

2. Use content not as a collection of isolated facts, but as a way for adolescents to critically think about the big questions.

3. Change the role of teacher from sole authoritarian to fellow traveler in search of knowledge.

4. Return the responsibility for learning to young people so they can understand their learning strengths and weaknesses and feel self-directed in their knowledge quest.[8]

---

8 Weimer, *Learner-Centered Teaching.*

3. The Role of the Teacher

We move into a role of coaching and mentoring young people to facilitate their own learning by designing experiences through which teenagers acquire knowledge and develop new skills. The goal of all teachers should be enabling others to be lifelong learners and giving them tools to succeed in this venture.

4. The Responsibility for Learning

We need to shift the responsibility for learning to young people. The primary goal of a teacher is to create a "climate for learning." Don't underestimate your power to model a passion for learning.

5. The Purpose and Processes of Evaluation

In this model, evaluation and purposes shift. It becomes less about people taking away our specific applications and more about a myriad of implications as they involve themselves in teaching and learning from each other. This method of learning is messy—a lot more like real life![9]

EXPERIENTIAL LEARNING CYCLE

Tell me and I'll forget; show me and I may remember; involve me and I'll understand.
—ANCIENT PROVERB

Learning is rooted in *experiencing* the information, not the information itself. Education pioneer John Dewey said, "There is an intimate and necessary relation between the processes of actual experience and education."[10] Dewey's writing and educational philosophy is the basis of many Western theories of education, and it largely shaped the Experiential Learning Cycle.

Developed by educational expert David Kolb in 1984, the Experiential Learning Cycle (sometimes called the Applied Learning Cycle) is the most widely used and accepted model in education describing the sequence and application of learning. Kolb said, "Learning is the process whereby knowledge is created through the transformation of experience."[11] The heart

---

9   Maryellen Weimer, *Learner-Centered Teaching: Five Key Changes to Practice* (San Francisco: Jossey-Bass, 2002).9 Weimer, Learner-Centered Teaching.

10 John Dewey, Experience and Education (New York: Simon & Schuster, 1938), 20.

11 David A. Kolb, *Experiential Learning: Experience as the Source of Learning and Development* (Upper Saddle River, NJ: Prentice Hall, 1984), 41.

of Kolb's model proposes four stages that move us toward applied learning: *Experience, Reflection, Conclusion, and Integration.*

I've adapted the wording and descriptions of these stages to offer some additional clarity and usefulness. I've also overlaid the segments of Bible Storying onto the diagram so you can see how it follows the Experiential Learning Cycle.

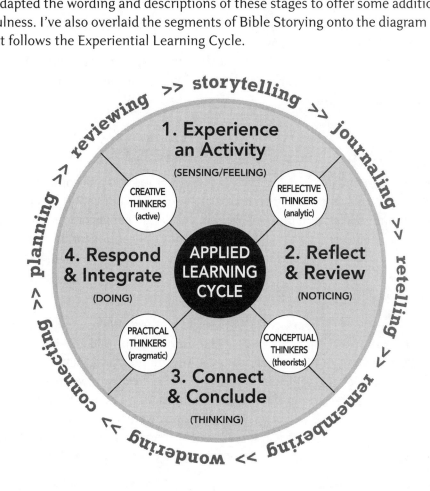

Kolb's model isn't just informative; it's also a helpful tool for evaluation. We can examine our ministries in light of this cycle, assessing whether or not we're balanced in providing learning opportunities in each stage. Investing in each stage of the cycle is critical, as the stages are interdependent and build upon each other. And each stage contributes to forming a foundation for subsequent learning. The other benefit of this cycle is that it connects with different types of processors at different stages. Following this cycle provides opportunities for reflective, conceptual, practical, and creative thinkers to engage and process along the way.

As teachers, we gravitate toward particular segments of the learning cycle. I know I could spend all day in the Process/Connecting segment—I love asking questions and letting ideas circulate. However, the danger in doing this is that if time is short, then we'll tend to focus only on our favorite parts of the cycle and cut short the rest. If we don't want to exclude certain types of learners from developing to their full potential, then we must practice giving emphasis to every part of the cycle.

BECOME AN EXPERIENCE ARCHITECT

One of the defining words for this digital era is *interactive*. We're becoming accustomed to being able to access and create our own media at a moment's notice. We desire to contribute to our own learning and entertainment like we would any conversation. We yearn to be a part of shared experiences. This desire has significant implications for the way we approach education. Places where we've traditionally accessed information—schools, libraries, and museums—have already observed this shift and moved toward making their learning opportunities more interactive.

There is a new set of standards for how we teach others. We're moving away from one-dimensional education with teachers being the experts who hold the key to information. Today's adolescents have instant access to most information, and they're becoming accustomed to being able to change, interact, and create while they learn. We teachers and leaders must become their guides to help them explore information and use it in the right context. This requires a new vision for our roles as educators as we become "experience architects," creating environments to help participants dive deeper and explore further into the things of God. This new role requires a significant investment of energy into creativity.

I hope this book will help you explore your new role as an experience architect. This adventure won't be easy. Teaching in new ways is unpredictable and unsettling, yet also full of wonder and moments of awakening. So we must move ahead into these uncharted waters, embarking on a new path of learning that asks a lot from us and from teenagers. And the reward of this adventure is great—a community of people who are transformed by God and ready to change the world. Together, may we enter the most amazing story ever told—God's Story.

HOW TO SET UP THE SEVEN EXPERIENCES

This book includes seven experiences to help you and the people you lead *enter* God's Story. These experiences will take you on a journey to explore some of the major milestones in the Bible, while helping your group learn, interact with, and place yourselves as a part of this continuing story.

These experiences offer multiple opportunities for solo and group learning, which are designed to help your group members get to know God, themselves, and each other in deeper ways. And each experience utilizes multiple stations or stopping points for groups to learn, interact, or pray.

IMPORTANT DETAILS

Make It Your Own—Feel free to change and shape these experiences to be your own. Improvise and get creative. Omit parts, add parts—whatever you need to do to connect with your group.

Test These Experiences Ahead of Time—especially the ones you're unsure about. It's better to run into problems a week in advance than discover a problem during the experience.

Group Sizes—For most of the experiences, the needed materials are appropriated for a group of approximately **eight people at each station** at one time. Please feel free to adjust the numbers according to your own needs. If you have a large group, you may want to replicate the stations so multiple groups of six to eight people can begin simultaneously. Another option would be to assign and schedule staggered group arrival times. However, keep in mind that these experiences follow a Bible narrative; therefore, most of the stations must be done in order.

Many of the stations include in-depth discussion and response times, which is why I strongly recommend an adult be a part of each group in order to help the group navigate any challenging points or to answer questions.

Duration—The experiences vary regarding how much time they'll take to complete—but most will take at least two hours. If you have a fixed ending time for your meeting, calculate how much time your group can spend at each station (the number of stations differs for each experience) and use a bell or other audible signal to prompt groups to move on to the next station. If you have tight time limitations, it might be best for you to split up the stations and do them over a series of weeks. You may want to provide a special area for groups to wait for their turn to begin the experience. Give them a selection of Scripture or other background information that relates to the experience that they can read together.

Assemble Your Team—A big part of this experience is creating it with others. Find people—adults or teenagers—who love to create environments through décor, lighting, fabric, art, and so on. Involve them early on in the process and ask them to help you create a vision for how you can make this experience your own. Involve others in the decorating, getting materials, organizing to-do lists, setting up the rooms, cleaning up, making music playlists, creating signs and art, whatever it takes.

ESSENTIAL MATERIALS

Files are available on the accompanying CD, including handouts, instructions, supply lists, signs, pictures, and images to help you create each experience. Most of these files are in PDF format.

OTHER USES

Many of the stations within each experience could stand alone as lessons for Sunday school classes or youth group meetings. And you could easily use these experiences as a series that's completed over several weeks.

Note: If you're "organizationally challenged" or not a detail person, then before you even begin find someone who will help you keep track of things. There are lots of materials and set-up needs for these experiences, and it takes a detailed eye to make it work well.

Creating Environments—In order to create an effective experience that will help teenagers enter the story, we must work hard at creating the right environments. It doesn't require a lot of money or materials to transform the feel of a space. But it does take people with the right eye for décor, know-how for creating the right vibe, and time to care for the small details. Find people who know how to use fabrics and candles to create a contemplative atmosphere.

Specific scenery or decor suggestions are given for each station as part of the materials lists. In creating these experiences, I tried to suggest everyday objects that are easily found, homemade, or inexpensive.

Each experience is divided into stations, stopping points where groups will learn, interact, or pray. Each station requires its own distinct area; most will require a table. Here are a few tips for creating the right environments:

- Use signage or masking tape arrows on the floor to direct participants to the next station.

- Use fabrics to cover tables and divide spaces. Talk to your local fabric or craft store about alerting you when they have closeouts or extra fabric available for bargain prices.

- Situate the stations fairly far apart to minimize distractions and allow room for several people at each station.

- Use lighting to set the mood. Turn off overhead lights and bring some lamps from home or find them cheap at Ikea. Use white Christmas lights.

- Candles are great—but be careful! Before you strike a match, check with the powers that be on any fire-code restrictions involving candles. If you aren't allowed to use candles, you can find electric ones that give off an authentic flicker. (Try www.batteryoperatedcandles.net) If you do use real candles, assign a helper to keep an eye on them, and never leave lit candles unattended.

- Instrumental music is a great way to create atmosphere. Keep the volume down and select music that is ambient.

RECOMMENDED MUSIC

The following is a playlist of music from my friends at Imago (www.imagocommunity.com). They're experts at creating environments and programming for events, and these songs are a great start for setting the right vibe. You should be able to sample and purchase any of these songs on iTunes.

ARTIST	SONG	ALBUM
Moby	"Chord Sounds"	Hotel
Brian Eno	"An Ending (Ascent)"	Apollo: Atmospheres & Soundtracks
Maurice Jarre	"Carpe Diem"	Dead Poets Society Soundtrack
Sigur Rós	"Takk…"	Takk…
Bill Frisell	"Over the Rainbow (Photo Book)"	Finding Forrester Soundtrack
Moby	"Inside"	Play
Hans Zimmer	"Elysium"	Gladiator Soundtrack
George Winston	"Black Stallion"	Summer
His Name Is Alive	"Sitting Still Moving Still Staring Outlooking"	Jerry Maguire Soundtrack

Hosts—give participants instructions, answer questions, replenish supplies, and keep things running smoothly. Hosts do not participate with the groups that go thorough the stations, but rather facilitate a smooth experience. Have hosts arrive early and do a walk-through of the station exercises to get a feel for them and catch if anything is missing.

Handouts—use for each station; they're available on accompanying CD. To save paper, some of the handouts instruct participants to leave the handout at the station. Because these experiences involve responsive readings and activities, there are a lot of handouts for each one. I've designed these events to be purposefully low-tech, releasing you from having to create video presentations and wrangle expensive equipment. These handouts contain all of the Scripture to be read aloud (lots of Scripture is included in each experience), thereby freeing participants' hands for interaction with tactile objects to enhance their learning.

Signage—Some stations may have signs or images to display. I often use old picture frames to display these. If you're going to hang things on the wall—be careful. Use blue painter's tape to protect painted surfaces or gaffer tape (like duct tape, but it doesn't leave a sticky residue) to hang heavier signage. When I set up these experiences, I often use signs on easels to delineate the stations. If you choose to do this, please add to your materials list an easel and a sign for each station. Your signage should be considered part of the experience, and you should try to make them a work of art. Have an artistic teen read through the handouts ahead of time and create a poster for each station—a painting, collage, and so on. Not only will this get more people involved, but it will also give a more creative and thoughtful look to your experiences.

KEEP A TRAVELOGUE

Consider giving each person in your group a journal as they begin these experiences. Ask them to journal their thoughts and dreams and prayers—to keep a *travelogue* that tells the story of their personal journey into God's Story.

Everyone Participates—Each experience is written with a similar rhythm, much like a liturgy or responsive reading. Segments are broken up for multiple people to read. Ask different teens and adults to read parts aloud. **When asking teenagers to read aloud, always ask for volunteers.** Forcing an adolescent to read could be a horrifying experience and cause that person to not want to participate in your group any longer. Group members who aren't reading will listen and follow the instructions given.

Pray! Pray as you set up and tear down, make prayer a regular part of creating these experiences. Ask God to help you and your group to be captured by theses stories and to find yourselves in them.

PART TWO
THE SEVEN EXPERIENCES

CREATION

DEVELOPED BY MICHAEL NOVELLI

*INSTRUCTIONS

DESCRIPTION

This experience is designed to help us imagine the creation story, igniting in each of us a sense of wonder and awe. Stations will move us from creative response to reflection and discussion about what it means for us to be created in God's image. The hope is that we'll be inspired by how awesome God is and see ourselves in a new light as image-bearers of God.

LOCATIONS AND LOGISTICS

Because this exercise follows the sequence of the creation narrative, it's best if the stations are done in order. Most of the stations could be done indoors or outdoors, except for Station 6, which requires participants to go for a walk outdoors. It's a good idea to do a walk-through ahead of time, so you can get a feel for what the participants will experience and make adjustments as needed.

REMINDER

Materials for each station are apportioned for a group of approximately eight people at one time. Please adjust according to your needs.

GROUP SIZE

Groups of six to eight move through the stations with a leader.

STATIONS (STOPPING POINTS)

INTRODUCTION

PREPARATION

Before you get started, make sure you have all the supplies you need for every station. Participants will gather around a table and pick up a key and a handout. Handouts will be returned to the table before the groups move on to the next station.

MATERIALS

- 10 Introduction handouts—returned by participants (available on accompanying CD).
- 12 or more different kinds of keys, the older the better.
- A long table.
- Old maps and Bibles to cover the table as decor.

STATION 1: CREATIVE BEGINNINGS

PREPARATION

Set up three areas for this station:

1. **Storytelling Area:** Participants sit in a circle—on couches or a big rug. This could be in a space that's separate from the other areas.
2. **Creative Response Area:** This station works best at a table where participants can create art.
3. **Art Display Area**: A place to hang art pieces and writings for others to view and reflect on. A creative way to do this is to stretch a rope across the room and hang the pieces with clothespins.

MATERIALS

- 10 Station 1 handouts—returned by participants (available on accompanying CD).

- One copy of the Beginnings Narrative handout (printed on a different color of paper than the Station 1 handouts) for the storyteller to read from—should be left at the station.

- CDs or MP3s of nature sounds (such as rushing water, wind, and so on) to play during the storytelling and a way to play them. Make sure the noises are subtle so they're not distracting.

- You could project stars onto the ceiling and darken the room for added effect. (For images or video loops of stars, search www.istock.com or go to your local library.)

- 10 Creative Response handouts (printed on a different color of paper than the Station 1 and Beginning Narrative handouts)—returned by participants (available on accompanying CD).

- Art supplies for the Creative Response area: Different kinds of paper, markers, colored pencils, scissors, and so on—enough for eight to 10 people.

- A table and table covering (to protect it from art supplies).

- Chairs for participants to use in the Creative Response area.

STATION 2: THE TRUTH ABOUT YOU

PREPARATION

This may work best in a room that's separate from the other stations and large enough for participants to spread out while they read and reflect. Place a large table (or tables) in the center of the room and cover it (them) with different kinds of mirrors.

MATERIALS

- Extra copies of the Station 2 handout—each participant gets to keep a copy (available on accompanying CD).

- A large table.

- Different shapes, sizes, and kinds of mirrors (enough to cover the large table).

- Dry erase markers—lots of colors.

- Optional: Small, mirrored tiles for each person to write on (To find inexpensive items like this, go to www.orientaltrading.com and search for "mirror tiles.").

STATION 3: FOOD AND FREEDOM

PREPARATION

There are two central items for this station: Fresh fruit to eat and The Tree of Life. The Tree of Life will also be used for Station 4, so you should place it in proximity to both stations.

MATERIALS

- 10 Station 3 handouts—returned by participants (available on accompanying CD).
- A variety of fresh fruit for participants to eat, displayed in bowls.
- Plates and napkins as needed.
- A table on which to place the fruit.
- The Tree of Life: This could be as simple as large tree branches attached to a base, a real tree, or a fake tree without leaves.[12]
- Leaf shapes made from colored paper—two for everyone (available on accompanying CD).
- Yarn or string for hanging the leaves on the tree.
- A single hole punch.
- Tape to affix yarn or string to the leaves.
- Markers for participants to write on the leaves.
- You may want to make your tree stand out even more by putting white Christmas lights on it.

STATION 4: PARTNERS WITH GOD

PREPARATION

Participants will need a table for drawing and writing. They'll also need a place to post their animal creation drawings after they're completed. These pieces could be combined with the art creations from Station 1.

---

12 The "Tree of Life" idea was appropriated from a similar idea on the Rethinking Youth Ministry blog at http://rethinkingyouth.blogspot.com/2009/02/ideas-for-lent-09-5-rest-stops.html.

MATERIALS

- 10 Station 4 handouts—returned by participants (available on accompanying CD).
- Paper, pens, and markers for pairs of participants to create their own animals.
- A table and chairs for participants to use.
- More leaf shapes—three to five leaves for each participant.
- Yarn or string to hang the leaves on the tree.
- A single hole punch.
- Tape to affix yarn or string to the leaves.
- Markers for participants to write on the leaves.
- The Tree of Life from Station 3 is used again—adding more leaves.
- A table containing gardening tools, packets of seeds, and other supplies.
- Optional: To make the table more "earthy," cover it with a tarp and put some mounds of potting soil on it for participants to run their hands through.

ADDITIONAL IDEAS

- Learn about and discuss some of the environmental crises in our world.
- Visit a greenhouse or botanical gardens and talk to a botanist about caring for plants and the plants' connection to the earth.
- Plant something in a local garden—either in pots or in the ground.

STATION 5: CREATED FOR RELATIONSHIPS

PREPARATION

Participants will create a paper chain, so allow space for it to grow.

MATERIALS

- 10 Station 5 handouts—returned by participants (available on accompanying CD).
- Precut strips of paper—each around eight to ten inches long and three to four inches wide—in a variety of colors. Cut at least two strips for each participant.

- A table and chairs for participants to use.

- Pens and markers.

- Scotch tape or staplers.

STATION 6: WALKING WITH GOD[13]

PREPARATION

This station works only outdoors, as it involves walking and observing nature. Have groups gather to read the handout and then head outside. Establish boundaries for the group members and a way to alert them when it's time to move on to the next station. If you haven't already, you should collect any cell phones, iPods, and gaming devices from the participants before they begin their walk.

MATERIALS

- 10 Station 6 handouts—returned by participants (available on accompanying CD).

STATION 7: RESTING IN GOD

PREPARATION

Use a large, open room with enough space for people to spread out, recline, and be at rest. Create a comfortable space with pillows, blankets, cushions, couches, rugs, and mats. You may even ask participants to bring along a pillow for this station. Hang some paper clouds around the room with verses printed on them for participants to meditate on.

MATERIALS

- 10 Station 7 handouts—returned by participants (available on accompanying CD).

- Pillows, blankets, cushions, couches, rugs, and mats.

- Subtle instrumental music to create a restful atmosphere.

- Cloud-shaped signs to hang from the ceiling or around the space with these verses printed on them:

13 Concept for this station adapted from Mark Yaconelli's *Downtime* (Zondervan/Youth Specialties, 2008), 211.

"Be still, and know that I am God." —PSALM 46:10

"Come to me, all you who are weary and burdened, and I will give you rest. Take my yoke upon you and learn from me, for I am gentle and humble in heart, and you will find rest for your souls. For my yoke is easy and my burden is light." —MATTHEW 11:28-30

There remains, then, a Sabbath-rest for the people of God; for those who enter God's rest also rest from their own work, just as God did from his. Let us, therefore, make every effort to enter that rest. —HEBREWS 4:9-11.

CREATION
Introduction

EVERYONE READ SILENTLY

This is an important time to…

- Connect with God and
- Connect with others in meaningful ways.

This time requires you to…

- Slow down and turn off your cell phone.
- Enter into a different pace of life.
- Speak quietly and act respectfully.
- Think deeply and engage your mind and heart.
- Be open to what God has for you.

We hope that through this experience you'll see how your story is connected to and a continuation of a bigger Story that began thousands of years ago.

Pray quietly and ask God to help you enter the story.

You will enter this experience in groups of six to eight people. At each station, different people from your group will read parts aloud. You don't have to read if you don't want to, but as many people as possible should read and help guide the experience.

*HANDOUTS

READER 1:

Pick up a key and put it in your hand. Take a deep breath and focus your heart and mind for the journey ahead. An important part of this journey is slowing down and working on the art of listening. Listen carefully to each other and to God. We begin this journey thinking about stories that have shaped our lives.

DISCUSS

- What is your favorite story from when you were growing up? (It could be from a book, a family story that's been passed down, or a movie.)

- What were your favorite characters from that story?

- Why did you love that story so much?

- How did it make you feel?

READER 2:

Everyone loves a good story. How many times has a movie, book, or song made you feel something? Something deep and meaningful? Something you couldn't even describe?

Stories have the power to take us on a journey.

They show us new places and introduce us to new people.

They draw us in…and we become a part of their adventure.

The best stories are the ones that show us something about ourselves.

They unveil to us more of who we are…and who we could become.

READER 3:

God's Story is like this.

It's a story full of mystery, action, miracles, war, drama, and love.

This story tells of a great and faithful Creator who reveals the best way to live…

A life of love, peace, and sacrifice.

It stretches from the beginning of time, across our lives, and into the future.

It begins with new life emerging…

> **In the beginning God created the heavens and the earth. —Genesis 1:1**

And moves to completion with new life emerging again…

> **"I am making everything new!" —Revelation 21:5**

READER 4:

God, the great Author, continues to write this Story and desires for us to find ourselves in it, discovering who we are, and why we're here.

If you will dive in and allow God to speak to you through the story, you'll see things about God—and yourself—that you've never seen before.

We're now going to enter the story of creation and see how it's a part of our own stories.

EVERYONE PRAY OUT LOUD

God, your story is amazing.

May we find our identities, purposes, and rest in your Story today.

Thank you for making all things new—including us.

Amen.

Please return your keys and put your handouts in a neat stack for the next group. Then continue on to the next station.

CREATION
Station 1
Creative Beginnings

SELECT A STORYTELLER

Who from your group can read a story with emotion and help bring it to life? Ask that person to be the storyteller for this station, reading the *Beginnings Narrative*.

READER 1:

Right now we're going to listen and respond to a paraphrased version of the creation story.

Those of us who've attended church for a long time will have to work extra hard at this and try to listen to this story as though it's the first time we've ever heard it. This will take concentration and something called "imaginative listening."

DISCUSS

What do you think it means to be an imaginative listener?

READER 2:

Since the creation of the universe is something beyond what we can capture in a movie or image, we'll use our image-making capacities—our imaginations—to enter into this story and watch it take shape in our minds. Let's imagine ourselves watching the story.

READER 3:

After we've finished listening to this story, we'll share what we noticed and then create something as a response.

If it helps you to concentrate, you may close your eyes during the story, write or draw, or choose a focal point to look at somewhere in the room.

Are you ready? Take a moment in silence to slow down and clear your mind. Whisper a prayer asking God to speak to *you* through the story.

Put your handouts in a neat stack for the next group.

"BEGINNINGS" NARRATIVE

This is a paraphrased version of the beginning of the creation story from Genesis 1–2 and Job 38. Designate a storyteller to read it aloud to the group...slowly—and twice.

Before anything existed there was The Creator…
A great and mysterious being called God.

While God was forming the Earth, the angels watched in amazement.
They sang and shouted together about how great God is!

With the angels cheering, God prepared the Earth as a place for life.

As God's Spirit moved over the dark and formless surface,
God spoke…and creation began taking shape.

God made light…pushing back the darkness…

Then God…separated the sky from the oceans and seas…
and gathered the waters, allowing dry land to surface…

God made plants, flowers, and trees grow—all with seeds in them so they could reproduce themselves. Water rose from the ground and nourished these plants.

Then God created the sun, the moon, and the universe that surrounds…
and set the seasons and time into motion…

And God filled the earth with all kinds of creatures…fish that swim in the seas,
birds that fly through the air, and wild animals that run and crawl across the land.

Looking at all of this wonderful creation, God thought, *This is really good!*

Leave this page at Station 1 for the next group.

CREATIVE CREATION RESPONSE

It's your turn to be creative! Take a few minutes to draw, paint, or write about the story images that stood out to you. Don't worry about creating something perfect or super-detailed—this is an act of personal expression and worship to God. While you're creating, talk about the following questions.

DISCUSS

- What did you see in your mind?

- What images stood out to you?

- Why do you think the angels cheered?

- What would it have been like to watch God create all of this?

- What did you notice for the first time in this story?

- How did God feel about creation? Why do you think God felt this way?

- What do you think is the most amazing and beautiful part of God's creation?

- What parts of creation do you like to visit?

After a few minutes, allow each person in your group who's willing to share what they created. If you have a designated Art Display Area, post your writings and artwork for others to reflect on.

After every willing person has shared, put your handouts in a neat stack for the next group. Then proceed to the next station.

CREATION
Station 2
The Truth about You

EVERYONE READ SILENTLY

Work through the study on the next few pages on your own. After about 15 minutes we will join together and discuss some of our thoughts.

In our struggle to find love and acceptance, we often place our worth in how we look, in our abilities, in how others treat us, or in what we do. Deep in our hearts we long to be loved for who we are. But we cannot see ourselves accurately. We must go to the One who created us and ask God to show us our real value. It's in God's infinite love that we begin to discover our true identities.

> **So God created human beings in his own image, in the image of God he created them; male and female he created them. —Genesis 1:27**

It's difficult for us to comprehend the idea that we're like God. We may have heard it said or read it a hundred times that we're "created in the image of God," but it seems unthinkable.

It can be especially difficult for us to see God's image in us through the pain and struggles we've faced. And it doesn't help that our society sends us messages that our self-worth comes from our looks, style, popularity, wealth, and abilities.

Thankfully, God has a different idea of who we are, and God desires for us to see ourselves as "image-bearers"—those who reflect God inside and out.

> **"The LORD does not look at the things human beings look at. People look at the out-ward appearance, but the LORD looks at the heart." —1 Samuel 16:7**

If we truly embrace the reality that we're made in God's image, it can transform our lives and turn our focus toward changing others' lives.

*HANDOUTS

YOUR IDENTITY

Read the following Bible passages slowly. Next to each passage, write down a word or phrase that stands out to you about God's love and your identity.

I will claim you as my own people, and I will be your God. Then you will know that I am the Lord your God who has freed you from your oppression in Egypt. —Exodus 6:7 (NLT)

You made me; you created me. Now give me the sense to follow your commands. —Psalm 119:73 (NLT)

So all of us who have had that veil removed can see and reflect the glory of the Lord. And the Lord—who is the Spirit—makes us more and more like him as we are changed into his glorious image. —2 Corinthians 3:18 (NLT)

Therefore, if anyone is in Christ, the new creation has come: The old has gone, the new is here! —2 Corinthians 5:17

We are therefore Christ's ambassadors, as though God were making his appeal through us. We implore you on Christ's behalf: Be reconciled to God. —2 Corinthians 5:20

So we are Christ's ambassadors; God is making his appeal through us. We speak for Christ when we plead, "Come back to God." —Ephesians 2:10 (NLT)

For in Christ all the fullness of the Deity lives in bodily form, and in Christ you have been brought to fullness. —Colossians 2:9-10a

CREATION Station 2: The Truth about You

Therefore, as God's chosen people, holy and dearly loved, clothe yourselves with compassion, kindness, humility, gentleness and patience. —Colossians 3:12

For God has not given us a spirit of fear and timidity, but of power, love, and self-discipline. —2 Timothy 1:7 (NLT)

Dear friends, since God loved us that much, we surely ought to love each other. No one has ever seen God. But if we love each other, God lives in us, and his love is brought to full expression in us. —1 John 4:11-12 (NLT)

JOURNAL

Now look back at what you wrote next to each of the verses and answer the following questions:

- Which of these is the most difficult for you to believe? Why do you have trouble seeing yourself this way?

- Which verses are most encouraging to you? Why?

*HANDOUTS

MIRROR IMAGES

Now pick three of the words that you wrote next to the verses above and write them on a mirror using the dry erase markers provided. As you do, take a moment to look at yourself in the mirror. See in your own eyes someone who's created in God's image and deeply loved.

> **We are not what we do. We are not what we have. We are not what others think of us. Coming home is claiming the truth. I am the beloved child of a loving Creator.**
> **—Henri Nouwen[14]**

The truth is that you're completely loved by God with a love that's greater than the love anyone in this world can offer you. God considers you to be valuable and worthy of his love. It's in God's limitless love that you must see yourself; this love must become your hope and identity.

Take a few moments and quiet your heart and mind. Block out all distractions.

Slowly read the following verses from Ephesians two or three times. And as you let the words soak in, pray and ask God to fill you with his amazing love.

> **I pray that from his glorious, unlimited resources he will empower you with inner strength through his Spirit. Then Christ will make his home in your hearts as you trust in him. Your roots will grow down into God's love and keep you strong. And may you have the power to understand, as all God's people should, how wide, how long, how high, and how deep his love is. May you experience the love of Christ, though it is too great to understand fully. Then you will be made complete with all the fullness of life and power that comes from God. —Ephesians 3:16-19 (NLT)**

DISCUSS

- How was this time meaningful for you? How were you encouraged?
- How did this station help change the way you look at yourself?

This handout is yours to keep. May it serve as a source of ongoing encouragement to you. Proceed to the next station.

14 Henri J.M. Nouwen, *Home Tonight: Further Reflections on the Parable of the Prodigal Son*, ed. Sue Mosteller, C.S.J. (DoubleDay, 2009), inside flap.

CREATION
Station 3
Food and Freedom

READER 1:

The story continues as God provides an amazing place for the first humans to live. This was a beautiful place full of really good food to eat!

> Now the LORD God had planted a garden in the east, in Eden; and there he put the man he had formed. The LORD God made all kinds of trees grow out of the ground—trees that were pleasing to the eye and good for food. —Genesis 2:8-9a

> Then God said, "I give you every seed-bearing plant on the face of the whole earth and every tree that has fruit with seed in it. They will be yours for food." —Genesis 1:29

READER 2:

Doesn't the garden sound like a place we'd all like to be right now? You probably noticed the delicious fruit sitting on the table in front of us. If you haven't already, take some fruit and enjoy it! As you eat, think about how God has provided for you—maybe in ways that you might normally take for granted.

(after a few minutes of eating, continue reading):

Each person should now pick up a paper leaf and a marker. Write on the leaf some ways that God has given you life and provided for you. After you're finished writing, attach a string to your leaf and hang it on the "Tree of Life."

READER 3: (after everyone has hung a leaf on the tree):

> In the middle of the garden were the tree of life and the tree of the knowledge of good and evil...And the LORD God commanded the man, "You are free to eat from any tree in the garden; but you must not eat from the tree of the knowledge of good and evil, for when you eat of it you will certainly die." —Genesis 2:9b, 16-17

*HANDOUTS

READER 4:

Humans were given the freedom to choose to listen to God or to follow their own ways. Without jumping ahead to the humans eating the fruit (in the next story), let's discuss this some more.

DISCUSS

- Why do you think God gave humans the freedom to make choices?

- What might this show us about God?

- What was God risking by giving us the ability to choose? What was there to gain?

READER 4: (after a brief discussion):

We could talk for a long time about the ideas of choice, freedom, and love. And as we continue to explore the creation story, more questions and wonderings than clear answers will probably surface. This is a good reminder that God is full of mystery—bigger and more amazing than we can fully understand.

Let's continue our journey at the next station. Please leave your handouts in a neat stack for the next group.

CREATION Station 3: Food and Freedom

LEAVES FOR COPYING AND CUTOUTS

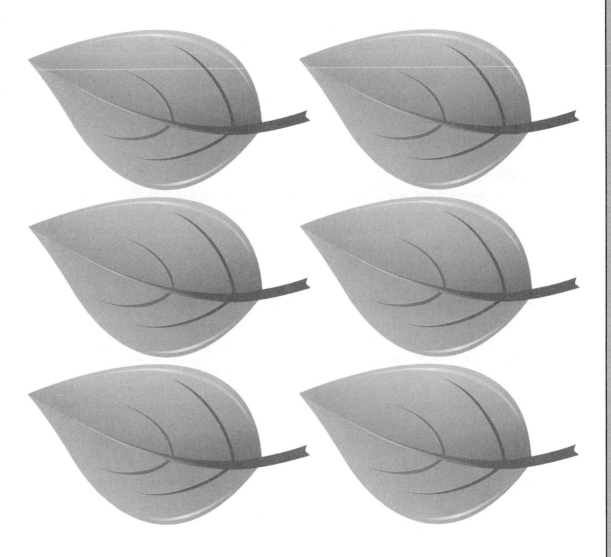

*HANDOUTS

CREATION
Station 4
Partners with God

READER 1:

> Now the LORD God had formed out of the ground all the wild animals and all the birds in the sky. He brought them to the man to see what he would name them; and whatever the man called each living creature, that was its name. So the man gave names to all the livestock, the birds in the sky and all the wild animals. —Genesis 2:19-20

CREATE YOUR OWN ANIMAL...

READER 2:

It must have been amazing (and possibly exhausting) to be the one who gave all the animals names. Now it's your turn to play both parts—creator and namer! With a partner, make up a new animal that's never been seen before. Draw a picture of it and be ready to share about its name, eating habits, and so on. Have fun! (By the way, the liger—the offspring of a male lion and a female tiger—has already been taken. And so has its opposite: The tigon.)

(after all of the pairs have shared about their creatures continue reading):

> Then God blessed them and said, "Be fruitful and multiply. Fill the earth and govern it. Reign over the fish in the sea, the birds in the sky, and all the animals that scurry along the ground." —Genesis 1:28 (NLT)

So humans aren't just another type of creature living on the earth. We've been given an amazing privilege to join with God in creating. We are co-creators in many ways—we create and sustain life by having children and caring for animals and plants. God has trusted us with a lot.

READER 3:

> The LORD God took the man and put him in the Garden of Eden to work it and take care of it. —Genesis 2:15

It would seem that work wasn't a struggle for the first humans, but it was a joy that gave them

CREATION Station 4: Partners with God

satisfaction and purpose. Humans were meant to carry on where God left off: Naming, creating, loving, ordering, enjoying, and resting. It's as though God is saying to us, "I put *you*, an image of myself, on the earth to continue all of the good I started."

DISCUSS

- If we're really an extension of God's care for all living things, then how should that change the way we live? How does that make you feel?

- God gave us plants, trees, water, animals, and air to sustain our lives. How have we taken these items for granted and not cared for them as well as we should?

- In what ways can we take better care of these things?

- How can we continue "all the good God has started" in our world and care for all living things?

- How can we better care for humans in need?

TURNING OVER A NEW LEAF

Come up with as many ideas as you can that would bring life to our world. Write them on the paper leaves. Then hang your leaves on the Tree of Life.

After everyone has finished hanging their leaves on the tree, put your handouts in a neat stack for the next group and continue on to the next station.

*HANDOUTS

CREATION
Station 5
Created for Relationships

READER 1:

Then the Lord God said, "It is not good for the man to be alone. I will make a helper who is just right for him"...Then the Lord God made a woman from the rib, and he brought her to the man. "At last!" the man exclaimed...This explains why a man leaves his father and mother and is joined to his wife, and the two are united into one. Now the man and his wife were both naked, but they felt no shame. —Genesis 2:18, 22, 23a, 24-25 (NLT)

READER 2:

Marriage is a beautiful picture of the intimacy we long for, where two people find in each other a missing part of themselves. We desire to live in close relationship—to know and be known by each other. We're designed to experience God within the deep bond of community.

JOURNAL

Journaling is an act of prayer. Hopefully it doesn't feel like an assignment, but it will be a way for you to express your heart to God. Pick up one of the colored strips of paper and take a moment to write down your responses to these questions in your journal:

- With whom do you share your hopes, dreams, fears, and worries? Write down their names.

- What kind of relationships do you desire right now?

- Write a short prayer asking God to bring the right people into your life.

READER 3 (after a minute or two of journaling):

God designed healthy relationships to be a partnership of mutual love and service. We discover true closeness and fulfillment when we become other-centered—instead of self-centered—working to listen to and care for each other unconditionally.

Do nothing out of selfish ambition or vain conceit. Rather, in humility value others above yourselves, not looking to your own interests but each of you to the interests of the others. —Philippians 2:3-4

The question, therefore, is not "How can we make community?" but "How can we develop and nurture giving hearts?" —Henri Nouwen[15]

Take another strip of paper and be ready to journal your responses to these next questions. But first, close your eyes and think about the faces of the people you see daily.

- Who is God bringing to mind that you could better serve with the love and humility of Christ? Write down their names.

- What are practical ways you could serve them? Write some ideas next to each name.

READER 4 (after a few minutes of journaling):

Now we're going to form a paper chain with our strips of paper. These "relationship links" may seem elementary, but a chain is a powerful metaphor for the wholeness and strength that we give and receive in our relationships. We're interconnected, relying on each other to grow in faith and face life's challenges.

Just as a body, though one, has many parts, but all its many parts form one body, so it is with Christ...Now you are the body of Christ, and each one of you is a part of it. —1 Corinthians 12:12, 27

JOIN YOUR LINKS

1. Thread your paper strip through another person's circle, then fasten its ends with tape or staples to make another interlinked circle.

2. Repeat until all of the group members' strips have been used. This will take some teamwork.

3. Link all of the groups' chains together and stretch it across the room.

*HANDOUTS

EVERYONE PRAY OUT LOUD

Join hands and read this prayer together:

> God,
> We're all grateful for the people you put into our lives who love and shape us.
> As we seek true intimacy and community,
> may we do that with you at the center of all of our relationships.
> Help us to grow in humility; fill us with love and eagerness to serve.
> May we find fulfillment in you and in the community that you surround us with.
> Amen.

Please put your handouts in a neat stack for the next group and continue on to the next station.

6 CREATION
Station 6
Walking with God

READER 1:

> Then the man and his wife heard the sound of the LORD God as he was walking in the garden in the cool of the day. —Genesis 3:8a

The image of God walking with humans in the cool of the day seems so peaceful. It also causes us to wonder what they talked about. The first humans probably had a lot of questions!

We're going to take time to walk with God like we would a close friend—just being together, listening, asking questions, and sharing our hearts.

> Walking slows us down to God's speed; walking in prayer gives way to strolling, meandering, and enjoying ourselves with God. —Mark Yaconelli[16]

READER 2:

> God saw all that he had made, and it was very good. —Genesis 1:31

Walk slowly and be aware of the sights and sounds of nature around you. Let your feet and hands feel the grass and the earth beneath you. Pick up a leaf, twig, or stone. As you feel the breeze, express your thankfulness for being a part of God's amazing creation.

This is a sacred time between you and God; conversations with the other people in your group will come later. Also, please stay within sight so we can let you know when to come back. *(Share any other details or boundaries that are important.)*

If you notice yourself getting distracted, simply pray and refocus, "Thank you God for walking with me."

Go and walk with God now.

Mark Yaconelli, Downtime: *Helping Teenagers Pray* (Zondervan/Youth Specialties, 2008), 210.

CREATION   53

*HANDOUTS

DISCUSS

- What sights, sounds, smells, and feelings stand out to you from your walk?

- How was this different than other times you've been on a walk?

- How did this time help you feel connected with God? How was it meaningful?

EVERYONE PRAY SILENTLY

In your own words, thank God for walking with you and for the amazing gift of creation that surrounds us.

Please put your handouts in a neat stack for the next group and continue on to the next station.

7 CREATION
Station 7
Resting in God

READER 1:

By the seventh day God had finished the work he had been doing; so on the seventh day he rested from all his work. Then God blessed the seventh day and made it holy, because on it he rested from all the work of creating that he had done. —Genesis 2:2-3

READER 2:

There remains, then, a Sabbath-rest for the people of God; for those who enter God's rest also rest from their own work, just as God did from his. Let us, therefore, make every effort to enter that rest. —Hebrews 4:9-11a

Our Creator knows each one of us deeply and intimately. God knows the hectic pace of our lives and how our lives are filled with distractions. We need rest. We need space to just BE.

READER 3:

"Be still, and know that I am God." —Psalm 46:10

We're going to take time in silence to slow down and allow God's love to wash over us. Make sure you find a spot that's comfortable, away from others and free from distractions. This is a time to rest our minds and bodies.

READER 4:

As we begin, take some deep, slow breaths. As you breathe out, release any distractions, worries, and tension to God. If it helps you, you may meditate on some of the verses that are posted, but don't feel obligated to *do* something—just *be* and enjoy God's presence.

"Come to me, all you who are weary and burdened, and I will give you rest. Take my yoke upon you and learn from me, for I am gentle and humble in heart, and you will find rest for your souls. For my yoke is easy and my burden is light." —Matthew 11:28-30

Let's spend some extended time now resting in God.

*HANDOUTS

DISCUSS

- How was this rest time meaningful for you? How did it help you feel connected to God?
- Think back through your experiences at all seven of the creation stations. What stands out to you? What was the most impactful?
- How did this experience challenge you to live differently?

After your discussion, please put your handouts in a neat stack for the next group.

DISRUPTION

DEVELOPED BY MICHAEL NOVELLI
WITH KELLY DOLAN & MARK NOVELLI

*INSTRUCTIONS

DESCRIPTION

The Disruption Experience helps your group dive into the stories of Adam and Eve, Cain and Abel, Noah, and the Tower of Babel. You will travel to three locations, and at each location participate in a different activity to help your group better understand and identify with these stories. The purpose of this experience is to explore disruption in our lives, relationships, and world, and see how God desires to bring restoration to those areas.

LOCATIONS AND LOGISTICS

This is different than most of the other experiences in this book in that it can be done with a larger group of up to 40 participants. Because this experience is based on a continuous Bible narrative, the stations must be done in order. Groups will visit a large tree, a cemetery, and a junkyard. It's a good idea to do a walk-through ahead of time so you can get a feel for what the participants will experience and make adjustments as needed.

GROUP SIZE

This can be done with a whole youth group. I recommend groups be no larger than 40 people, as it may be hard to hear one another and discuss.

STATIONS (STOPPING POINTS)

STATION 1: IDENTITY CRISIS

LOCATION

The group will sit in a tight circle around a large tree.

MATERIALS

- An apple for every person.
- Copies of the Station 1 handout—to be kept by participants (available on accompanying CD).
- Optional: A pencil or pen for each person.

STATION 2: RELATIONAL BREAKDOWN

LOCATION

Take the group to visit a local cemetery.

MATERIALS

- Copies of the Station 2 handout—to be kept by participants (available on accompanying CD).

STATION 3: GLOBAL DISRUPTION

LOCATION

Meet in a junkyard or in view of a landfill or some run-down buildings.

MATERIALS

- Copies of the Station 3 handout—to be kept by participants (available on accompanying CD)
- Images of global disruption and brokenness—one for every group of three—such as child labor, slavery, pollution, poverty, violence and war, broken families, greed, vanity, loneliness, and starvation (recommended images to purchase from iStock Photo are available on accompanying CD). Different groups can use the same image, if needed.

DISRUPTION
Introduction

EVERYONE READ SILENTLY

This is an important time to…

- Connect with God and
- Connect with others in meaningful ways.

This time requires you to…

- Slow down and turn off your cell phone.
- Enter into a different pace of life.
- Speak quietly and act respectfully.
- Think deeply and engage your mind and heart.
- Be open to what God has for you.

We hope that through this experience you'll see how your story is connected to and a continuation of a bigger Story that began thousands of years ago.

Pray quietly and ask God to help you enter the story.

You will enter this experience with your entire group. At each station, different people from your group will read parts aloud. You don't have to read if you don't want to, but as many people as possible should read and help guide the experience.

READER 1:

You may be wondering why this group experience is called "Disruption." What do you think of when you hear that word? *(Allow time for a couple of responses.)*

To *disrupt* means "to throw something into confusion or disorder; to interrupt or impede the progress of something."[17]

*HANDOUTS

The creation story from the Bible tells us that the first humans experienced complete harmony with God. Things were in their right places, and they lived in rhythm with God's goodness. But human selfishness broke that harmony, disrupting God's kingdom ways on earth and in their hearts.

We're now going to reenter this story and explore areas of disruption in our lives, relationships, and world.

THE GROWING PROBLEM OF DISRUPTION

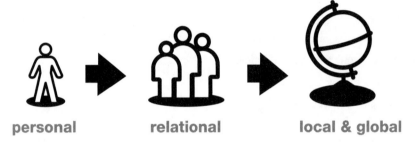

personal   relational   local & global

READER 2:

We'll dive into the stories of Adam and Eve, Cain and Abel, Noah, and the Tower of Babel. We'll travel to three locations, and at each location we'll participate in a different activity to help us better understand and identify with these stories. If we look closely, we'll see parts of ourselves everywhere in these stories.

Throughout this experience, ask yourself:

- What would it have been like to actually be in these stories?

- How am I like the characters in the stories?

- How are these stories challenging me to think and live differently?

Are you ready to get started on our journey? ***You may keep this handout.***

DISRUPTION
Station 1
Identity Crisis

Find a large tree nearby. Sit in a tight circle either around or near the tree so you can all hear each other.

READER 1:

The creation story paints a picture of humans, God, and nature all living in perfect harmony. Close your eyes. Take a moment to replay in your mind the story of creation. *(Pause for a moment.)*

DISCUSSION

- What do you remember about the story?

- What do you see in your mind when you think of the creation story?

- How does this story make you feel?

READER 2:

The creation story begins with God, the Great Creator, taking the Earth—which was only a mass of darkness and chaos—and preparing it as a place for life. Then God created all kinds of living creatures and natural wonders.

Distinct creatures—called "human beings"—were formed to reflect God's image. And God shared a close relationship with these humans, walking with them in the cool of the day.

Humans were also given the great joy of continuing God's work, creating and caring for all living things. They lived in God's kingdom ways—a life that was whole and complete.

DISCUSS

- How do you think the story of creation gives us a glimpse into our true identities?

- How were we designed to live?

DISRUPTION Station 1: Identity Crisis

After a few minutes of discussion, pass out the apples but instruct the group not to eat them yet!

READER 3:

The serpent was the shrewdest of all the wild animals the Lord God had made. One day he asked the woman, "Did God really say you must not eat the fruit from any of the trees in the garden?"

"Of course we may eat fruit from the trees in the garden," the woman replied. "It's only the fruit from the tree in the middle of the garden that we are not allowed to eat. God said, 'You must not eat it or even touch it; if you do, you will die.'"

"You won't die!" the serpent replied to the woman. "God knows that your eyes will be opened as soon as you eat it, and you will be like God, knowing both good and evil."
—Genesis 3:1-5 (NLT)

READER 4:

The woman was convinced. She saw that the tree was beautiful and its fruit looked delicious, and she wanted the wisdom it would give her. So she took some of the fruit and ate it. Then she gave some to her husband, who was with her, and he ate it, too. At that moment their eyes were opened, and they suddenly felt shame at their nakedness. So they sewed fig leaves together to cover themselves. When the cool evening breezes were blowing, the man and his wife heard the Lord God walking about in the garden. So they hid from the Lord God among the trees.
—Genesis 3:6-8 (NLT)

READER 5:

This is a strange story with its talking serpents and forbidden fruit. It's easy for us to focus on the seemingly surreal nature of the story and not explore the deeper meaning. Yet, it can help us discover profound things about what's gone wrong with our world and ourselves.

DISCUSS

- What do you think it means that Adam and Eve desired to "be like God"?

- How is this different than being made in God's image?

- What usually happens when humans decide for themselves what's good or evil, right or wrong?

- Humans desire autonomy. How can this desire be complex and difficult?

- Can we ever be free from external control or influences? Explain.

AUTONOMY

Freedom from external control or influence;[18] self-directing freedom and especially moral independence.[19]

- What do you think God was (is) trying to protect the humans from?

- How did the first humans react immediately after they ate the fruit? How did they feel? Why?

- In what ways did the first humans disregard their true identities in God?

READER 6:

Look at the apple in your hand. It represents our daily choices to follow our ways or God's. Bite into the apple and remain silent for a few moments. As you eat the apple, think about:

- The poor decisions you've made recently that are causing regret and hurt

- The lies you're believing about yourself that God wants you to ignore

- How you're living outside of your true identity in God

(after a minute or two of silence continue reading):

Spend some time quietly confessing to God the areas in which you've chosen your own ways over God's. Use this time to ask God for forgiveness and strength.

If you like, you can journal your prayers on the back of your handout or in your own journal. In about five minutes, we'll travel to the next location. You may keep this handout.

New Oxford American Dictionary, ## ed., s.v. "Autonomy."
Merriam-Webster's Online Dictionary, s.v. "Autonomy." http://www.merriam-webster.com/dictionary/autonomy

*HANDOUTS

Now you'll visit a local cemetery. Find a place in the cemetery where your group can stand in a circle. This should be a quiet place where you can easily see some headstones.

This is a time for reflection and serious thought. Please don't run around, sit on the headstones, or play in the cemetery. Be respectful.

READER 1:

When the cool evening breezes were blowing, the man and his wife heard the Lord God walking about in the garden. So they hid from the Lord God among the trees. Then the Lord God called to the man, "Where are you?"

He replied, "I heard you walking in the garden, so I hid. I was afraid because I was naked."

"Who told you that you were naked?" the Lord God asked. "Have you eaten from the tree whose fruit I commanded you not to eat?"

The man replied, "It was the woman you gave me who gave me the fruit, and I ate it."

Then the Lord God asked the woman, "What have you done?"

"The serpent deceived me," she replied. "That's why I ate it." —Genesis 3:8-13 (NLT)

READER 2:

Then God said to the woman, "I will sharpen the pain of your pregnancy, and in pain you will give birth. And you will desire to control your husband, but he will rule over you."

And to the man God said, "Since you listened to your wife and ate from the tree whose fruit I commanded you not to eat, the ground is cursed because of you. All your life you will struggle to scratch a living from it. It will grow thorns and thistles for you, though you will

eat of its grains. By the sweat of your brow will you have food to eat until you return to the ground from which you were made.

For you were made from dust, and to dust you will return." —Genesis 3:16-21 (NLT)

DISCUSS

- How did the humans respond when confronted with their rebellion? Why do you think they responded this way?

- Why do you think the humans were full of shame and fear?

- How did Adam and Eve's relationships with God change? With each other? With the earth?

- How did God still show Adam and Eve care in the midst of their shame?

READER 3:

Things changed drastically for Adam and Eve. Their new awareness of evil brought with it a sense of insecurity, shame, and defensiveness. The humans pointed fingers at each other and fought to control their relationship. In a real way, they experienced the beginnings of death in their broken relationships with God, each other, and the world.

Unfortunately, things got worse between Adam and Eve's sons, Cain and Abel. Within just the first family we see humans struggling with insecurity, jealousy, hatred, comparison, deception, and murder.

READER 4:

When they grew up, Abel became a shepherd, while Cain cultivated the ground. When it was time for the harvest, Cain presented some of his crops as a gift to the Lord. Abel also brought a gift—the best of the firstborn lambs from his flock. The Lord accepted Abel and his gift, but he did not accept Cain and his gift. This made Cain very angry, and he looked dejected.

"Why are you so angry?" the Lord asked Cain. "Why do you look so dejected? You will be accepted if you do what is right. But if you refuse to do what is right, then watch out! Sin is crouching at the door, eager to control you. But you must subdue it and be its master."

One day Cain suggested to his brother, "Let's go out into the fields." And while they were in the field, Cain attacked his brother, Abel, and killed him.

Afterward the Lord asked Cain, "Where is your brother? Where is Abel?" "I don't know," Cain responded. "Am I my brother's guardian?"

But the Lord said, "What have you done? Listen! Your brother's blood cries out to me from the ground!" —Genesis 4:2b-10 (NLT)

DISCUSS

- What feelings motivated Cain toward violence?
- Which of these characters are you sometimes like? How?
- How do we allow our desires to disrupt and destroy our relationships?

READER 5:

Our selfishness and desire for control brings about death in many ways—physical, emotional, environmental, spiritual. When we choose our own ways instead of God's, it leads to a life of pain, struggle, and loneliness. We miss out on life the way it's designed to be.

For the next 10 minutes, I want you to slowly and silently walk around the cemetery by yourself. But stay within eyesight of the group. Read through the questions provided, pray, and think deeply about the people God has put into your life.

EVERYONE READ SILENTLY

1. As you slowly walk, picture in your mind the people who bring life to you. Who takes care of you? Encourages you? Gives you good advice? Laughs and cries with you? As you picture these people, whisper their names aloud and thank God for their lives.

DISRUPTION Station 2: Relational Breakdown

2.   Now picture the people who cause you frustration, jealousy, or hurt. This could be a parent, friend, brother or sister, coworker, or classmate. As you picture these people, pray for them. Ask God to forgive you for the ways you've mistreated others. Ask God to change your heart toward them and forgive them. Ask God to fill you with love, compassion, patience, and strength.

3.   Look at the gravestones. Think about the lives and families of the people buried here. On each gravestone there are birth and death dates. In between those numbers is a dash. That dash represents a life. As you pause at a few gravestones, think about how you want to spend *your* life. Ask God to shape you into a person who brings life to others.

DISCUSS (AFTER 10 MINUTES OF SILENT PRAYER)

-   How was this meaningful for you?

-   What kinds of relationships do you think God intends for you to have with this group?

READER 1:

Sit in a close circle together. Look at those around you. These are your brothers and sisters. Look closely. This may be hard to do without laughing, but really look at the people God has put into your life.

Our group isn't perfect, but we've been given a chance to move beyond our insecurities, pride, and fear and reflect a loving community in action. This will take all of us moving beyond what's comfortable, being vulnerable and humble, and reaching out to care for each other.

Maybe there's someone in our group whom you need to ask to forgive you. You may have mistreated or ignored that person. Don't let it go. Make time to restore that relationship so it doesn't continue to create disruption in your heart and in our group.

Now we're going to quietly pray for each other. Place your hands on the shoulders of the two people sitting next to you. Whisper a prayer asking God to fill them with love and to help them bring life to others around them.

After a few minutes of quiet prayer, continue on to the next location. You may keep this handout.

DISRUPTION
Station 3
Global Disruption

Visit a local junkyard, run-down area, or landfill—but stand at a distance so the group remains safe.

READER 1:
Just a few generations after Cain and Abel, humans were completely out of control, continually acting out in selfishness and violence.

Please close your eyes as I read these verses two times.

The LORD saw how great the wickedness of the human race had become on the earth, and that every inclination of the thoughts of the human heart was only evil all the time. The LORD regretted that he had made human beings on the earth, and his heart was deeply troubled. So the LORD said, "I will wipe from the face of the earth the human race I have created—and with them the animals, the birds and the creatures that move along the ground—for I regret that I have made them"…Now the earth was corrupt in God's sight and was full of violence. God saw how corrupt the earth had become, for all the people on earth had corrupted their ways. —Genesis 6:5-7, 11-12

DISCUSS

- Where did human rebellion begin? How do you think it got so much worse?

- What do you think motivated people to act this way?

- Where have you seen violence spiral out of control around you? In our world?

- How do you think one act of violence or selfishness leads to another?

- What might that tell us about our own rebellion and selfishness?

- How do you think human rebellion escalates worldwide into poverty, slavery, war, homelessness, injustice, pollution, starvation, and so on?

READER 2:

The selfish decisions of humans have seemingly snowballed into an avalanche of disruption and chaos. Human desire for power triggered a downward spiral of brokenness, rebellion, and pain that reverberates today. Everyone and everything in our world is affected by this disruption.

READER 3:

Even after a flood devastated the whole earth, it didn't take long for humans to forget their identity as image-bearers of God.

> Now the whole world had one language and a common speech. As people moved eastward, they found a plain in Shinar and settled there. They said to each other, "Come, let's make bricks and bake them thoroughly." They used brick instead of stone, and tar for mortar. Then they said, "Come, let us build ourselves a city, with a tower that reaches to the heavens, so that we may make a name for ourselves and not be scattered over the face of the whole earth."
>
> But the LORD came down to see the city and the tower that they were building. The LORD said, "If as one people speaking the same language they have begun to do this, then nothing they plan to do will be impossible for them. Come, let us go down and confuse their language so they will not understand each other."
>
> So the LORD scattered them from there over all the earth, and they stopped building the city. That is why it was called Babel—because there the LORD confused the language of the whole world. From there the LORD scattered them over the face of the whole earth. —Genesis 11:1-9

DISCUSS

- What motivated the people to build a great tower?
- How was this destructive? Why did God stop them?
- How do people in our world today build "towers" to themselves?
- How do people strive for fame?

*HANDOUTS

READER 4:

We were designed to partner with God and care for all living things. It seems that in our obsession for control and power, we forget who we are and the way things should be.

DISCUSS

- Why do you think we came to a place like this?

- Look around you…how are things different here than the way God intended for them to be?

- How does this place seem disrupted and broken?

- How do you think we got so far from where we started?

READER 5:

As followers of Jesus, we have the great privilege to join with God and bring restoration to a hurting world. When we see people and places disrupted from how they were created to be, we're to come together and bring hope, healing, and justice.

Get in groups of three. Each group will receive an image to discuss and pray for. *(Hand out the images.)* These images represent ways that humans have forgotten who we are—disrupting and destroying relationships and the world around us.

Take a moment to pass the image around your group of three. Then discuss:

- Where in our world have I seen this problem?

- What human attitudes and actions lead to this problem?

- How have I contributed to this problem?

- How can we help solve this problem and bring restoration locally? Around the world?

After about five minutes, gather everyone back together in a big circle.

DISRUPTION Station 3: Global Disruption

DISCUSS

- How was this meaningful for you?
- How could we bring restoration to our area and to the world?

READER 6:

After the great flood, God gave Noah and his family a special promise:

> **"Whenever I bring clouds over the earth and the rainbow appears in the clouds, I will remember my covenant between me and you and all living creatures of every kind."**
> **—Genesis 9:14-15a**

A rainbow is a sign of hope, a reminder of God's continual love and desire to restore all things back to the way they were designed.

Let's spend some time in a circle praying and thanking God together. Let's thank God for always providing a way for us and for giving us hope. Share out loud how God has specifically given you hope. Ask God to bring restoration to your life, relationships, and our world.

You may keep this handout.

EXPERIENCE THREE

ISRAEL'S JOURNEY

DEVELOPED BY MICHAEL NOVELLI
WITH KELLY DOLAN

*INSTRUCTIONS

DESCRIPTION

Israel's Journey helps your group to dive into some of the key stories of the Hebrew people. You'll walk to 10 different stations, and at each location you'll participate in a different activity to help your group better understand and identify with these stories. The purpose of this experience is to learn more about our spiritual ancestors, get a feel for their journey, and see how this story connects to Jesus, the church, and our own stories.

LOCATIONS AND LOGISTICS

- This experience requires pleasant (i.e., warm and dry) weather. Stations 1 and 10 can be done indoors in the same room, and Stations 2 through 8 are done outdoors.

- For Stations 2 through 8, find a large open space, like a park, with few distractions. This area must have a bridge preferably with some kind of body of water underneath it—a creek or pond will suffice. (A bridge of some kind without water underneath will do as well.)

- Create two large signs to place on either side of the bridge. The sign closest to where you begin should read: THE PROMISED LAND. The sign on the opposite side should read, SLAVERY, WANDERING, & EXILE. You could affix these to sawhorses or real estate sign holders.

- I've provided a sketch of a very basic aerial map to give you an idea of how this experience might look.

- It's a good idea to do a walk-through ahead of time, so you can get a feel for what the participants will experience and make adjustments as needed.

- Important: Ask participants to wear comfortable shoes and clothes for walking a long distance. Also, they must bring an empty bag or piece of luggage with them for the experience. They will be carrying this bag filled with several items (that you'll provide) for the duration. This ties into the theme of journey and wandering. Bring extra luggage for participants who forget to bring their own.

GROUP SIZE

This can be done with a whole group. I recommend groups are no larger than 40 people at once, as it may be hard to hear one another during the discussion times.

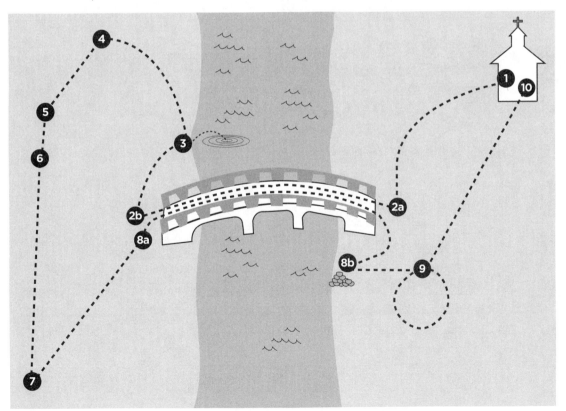

STATIONS (STOPPING POINTS)

STATION 1: COVENANT

LOCATION AND PREPARATION

The first station will most likely be located at your church. Participants will write on each other's wrists the word *blessing* with a dry erase marker. Then have them put a dry erase marker in their bags for the remainder of the journey. Hand out the rest of the supplies that are required for this experience at the first station and have participants put them in their bags.

JOURNEY SUPPLIES

Provide these items—one for each person:

- A dry erase marker—darker colors.
- A bottle of drinking water.
- A piece of sour candy or fruit.
- A large stone—could be as big as a grapefruit.
- A piece of sweet candy or a doughnut. (Keep in mind the dietary restrictions of your participants.)
- A small chunk of modeling clay or Play-Doh.
- A small sandwich bag for the clay. (Trust me, this will prevent a mess!)
- An individually wrapped Wet-Nap.
- A small-to-medium-sized smooth stone—should fit in one hand.
- A Sharpie marker.
- Copies of the station handouts for each participant to keep (available on accompanying CD).
- Optional: A journal and something to write with.

MATERIALS

- A video projector (with computer connection) to project stars on the ceiling.

- A digital image of stars. (For images or video loops of stars, search www.istock.com or go to your local library.)

- Copies of the Station 1 handout for each participant (available on accompanying CD) in their bags.

COULD I DO THIS EXPERIENCE AT NIGHT?

I've wondered what this experience would be like if it were done at night. If it were dark outside, the first station could be done outdoors, assuming you could see stars in the sky. Then participants would need to bring flashlights to read the handouts and light their way. Sounds like a cool idea, but it adds some extra risk. It's easier for your participants to wander off at night!

STATION 2: SLAVERY

LOCATION AND PREPARATION

Depending on the outdoor location you've chosen, you'll either walk or drive to the area you've designated as "The Promised Land." This should be an area close to a bridge that spans some water. (Again, it's okay if it's a bridge without water underneath, too.) Ahead of time or right when you arrive, designate this area with a sign. Participants will cross the bridge to another area you've designated as "Slavery, Wandering, & Exile."

MATERIALS

- Create two large signs to place on each side of the bridge. The sign closest to where you begin should read THE PROMISED LAND. The sign for the farther side should read SLAVERY, WANDERING, & EXILE. You could affix these signs to sawhorses or real estate sign holders.

- A bottle of water (in their bags).

- A piece of sour candy or fruit (in their bags).

- Copies of the Station 2 handout for each participant to keep (available on accompanying CD) (in their bags).

STATION 3: EXODUS

LOCATION AND PREPARATION

Your group will walk a little ways and find a spot overlooking the water. Here you'll reflect on and discuss the Israelites' slavery and exodus from Egypt. To signify liberation (theirs and ours), participants will throw the large stone they've been carrying in their packs into the water.

Note: For most of the stations, there are no designated distances for how far you should walk. Therefore, it's a good idea to do a walk-through ahead of time so you can get a feel for what the participants will experience and make adjustments as needed. (You won't cross the bridge back to "The Promised Land" until Station 8.)

MESSIANIC SEDER

A great way to go deeper into the exodus story is to host a Seder. I've hosted numerous Seders with groups, and I've created a resource for you to use at www.echothestory.com—click on Resources.

MATERIALS

- A large stone (in their bags).
- Copies of the Station 3 handout for each participant to keep (available on accompanying CD) (in their bags).

STATION 4: COMPLAINING

LOCATION AND PREPARATION

Your group will walk a few blocks away from the last station and away from the water. You must do this without crossing the bridge and going back into the "Promised Land" area.

MATERIALS

- A sweet treat (in their bags).
- Copies of the Station 4 handout for each participant to keep (available on accompanying CD) (in their bags).

STATION 5: RHYTHM OF LIFE

LOCATION AND PREPARATION

Your group will walk about one block to an open area and try to envision themselves at the base of a large mountain.

MATERIALS

- A dry erase marker (in their bags).
- Copies of the Station 5 handout for each participant to keep (available on accompanying CD) (in their bags).

STATION 6: IDOLS

LOCATION AND PREPARATION

Your group will walk about 100 feet from the previous station.

MATERIALS

- A sandwich bag containing a small chunk of modeling clay or Play-Doh (in their bags).
- An individually wrapped Wet-Nap (in their bags).
- Copies of the Station 6 handout for each participant to keep (available on accompanying CD) (in their bags).

STATION 7: WANDERING

LOCATION AND PREPARATION

Your group will walk about four to six blocks away from the last station and away from the bridge. After some brief readings, participants will get in groups of two and discuss the questions as they walk back toward the bridge. Participants won't cross the bridge, however, until the next station.

THE TABERNACLE

A great way to go deeper into the wanderings story is to find a place to insert the Tabernacle Experience (found in Part Two of this book, Experience Four).

*INSTRUCTIONS

MATERIALS

- Copies of the Station 7 handout for each participant to keep (available on accompanying CD) (in their bags).

STATION 8: ENTERING THE PROMISED LAND

LOCATION AND PREPARATION

Your group will cross the bridge back into the Promised Land and build a small monument near the water using the small stones in their packs.

MATERIALS

- A small-to-medium-sized smooth stone (in their bags).
- A Sharpie marker (in their bags).
- Copies of the Station 8 handout for each participant to keep (available on accompanying CD) (in their bags).

STATION 9: A VICIOUS CYCLE AND EXILE

LOCATION AND PREPARATION

Your group will walk in a big circle together. The second time you do this, you'll stop halfway around and discuss the Israelites' vicious cycle. Directions for this are a bit more involved than for other stations, so make sure you walk through them ahead of time.

MATERIALS

- Copies of the Station 9 handout for each participant to keep (available on accompanying CD) (in their bags).

STATION 10: FUTURE HOPE

LOCATION AND PREPARATION

Your group will travel back to the same location as the first station. This will most likely be at your church. Together you'll light some candles, so it would be good if this would take place in a room without much light to add to the effect.

MATERIALS

- A seven-candle menorah or seven individual candles positioned close together.
- Copies of the Station 10 handout for each participant to keep (available on accompanying CD) (in their bags).

ISRAEL'S JOURNEY
Introduction

EVERYONE READ SILENTLY

This is an important time to...

- Connect with God and

- Connect with others in meaningful ways.

This time requires you to...

- Slow down and turn off your cell phone.

- Enter into a different pace of life.

- Speak quietly and act respectfully.

- Think deeply and engage your mind and heart.

- Be open to what God has for you.

We hope that through this experience you'll see how your story is connected to and a continuation of a bigger Story that began thousands of years ago.

Pray quietly and ask God to help you enter the story.

You will enter this experience with your entire group. At each station, different people from your group will read parts aloud. You don't have to read if you don't want to, but as many people as possible should read and help guide the experience.

READER 1:

Today, we'll have a chance to glimpse the journey of the Israelites. We'll put ourselves in the stories of Abraham and Moses and imagine what it was like to be one of the Hebrew people. Their journeys were filled with miracles, tragedies, and struggles. If we look closely, we can easily see ourselves in these stories as people who wrestle with our own faith and direction.

This experience will involve going on a long walk and stopping at various points to learn about and discuss the story of the Israelites' journey.

Throughout this experience, ask yourself…

- What would it have been like to be a part of these stories?

- How am I like the characters in these stories?

- How are these stories challenging me to think and live differently?

READER 2:

Before we begin, make sure you have all of the necessary supplies for your journey.

Each of you should have a bag or piece of luggage containing the following items:

- A dry erase marker
- A piece of sour candy or fruit
- A piece of sweet candy or a doughnut
- A small chunk of modeling clay or Play-Doh
- A small sandwich bag for the clay
- A copy of each of the station handouts (10 total)

- A bottle of drinking water
- A large stone
- An individually wrapped Wet-Nap
- A Sharpie marker
- A small smooth stone
- A journal (optional)

You'll be carrying your own bag for the entire experience. Please wait to remove any items from your bag until you've been instructed to do so.

You may keep this handout. Now continue on to the first station.

*HANDOUTS

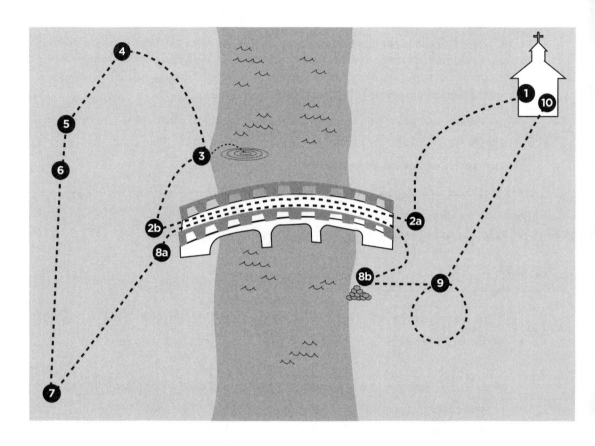

ISRAEL'S JOURNEY
Station 1
Covenant

As you enter, find a comfortable spot to sit quietly, listen, and look up at the stars.

READER 1:

Thousands of years ago, God made a commitment—called a *covenant*—with a man named Abraham, saying…

> The Lord had said to Abram, "Leave your native country, your relatives, and your father's family, and go to the land that I will show you. I will make you into a great nation. I will bless you and make you famous, and you will be a blessing to others. I will bless those who bless you and curse those who treat you with contempt. All the families on earth will be blessed through you." —Genesis 12:1-3 (NLT)

Read these verses again.

DISCUSS

- The word *covenant* means "joining together," representing a deep, binding promise of commitment.

- What was God promising to do?

- Why would God make a covenant with humans? What do you think this shows us about God?

READER 2:

The Hebrew word for "bless" that's used in these verses is *barak*. The primary meaning of this word is to give something of value. *Barak* is also rooted in the Hebrew word for *knee*, a reminder that serving and giving is to be done with humility and gratitude.

> [Jesus said,] "You have heard that it was said, 'Love your neighbor and hate your enemy.' But I tell you, love your enemies! Pray for those who persecute you!" —Matthew 5:43-44

*HANDOUTS

"For even the Son of Man came not to be served but to serve others and to give his life as a ransom for many."—Matthew 20:28 (NLT)

DISCUSS

- How do we curse someone? Why is this easier than blessing a person?

- According to the meaning of the word *barak*, what does it mean for us to "bless" others?

- What do you think it means for you to be God's blessing to the world? What are some specific ways that we could live this out?

NOTE: We'll be using the names *Hebrews*, *Israelites*, *People of Israel*, and *Jews* interchangeably as we describe God's people who descended from Abraham and have followed the Jewish faith throughout the centuries.

READER 3:

Close your eyes and breathe deeply. Think of the people you see every day. Picture their faces in your mind. Whom have you ignored or been harsh with? Whom have you encouraged or blessed recently? Pray for them and ask God to be a blessing in their lives from this point forward.

(continue reading after a few minutes of prayer):

As I read these verses, look up at the stars and imagine what it would have been like to be there with Abraham.

> Then the LORD took Abram outside and said to him, "Look up into the sky and count the stars if you can. That's how many descendants you will have!" And Abram believed the LORD, and the LORD counted him as righteous because of his faith. —Genesis 15:5-6 (NLT)

This was an amazing promise—God chose to extend his blessing through one man who'd grow into a nation and later connect to a movement of people worldwide called the church.

For Abraham is the father of all who believe. —Romans 4:16b (NLT)

We're a part of this story—called to show the world what it means to live in God's ways and extend God's blessing to everyone we meet.

REFLECT

Take a dry erase marker (not the Sharpie) and ask a friend to write the word BLESSING on your right wrist. Make sure you put the marker back in your bag for the remainder of the journey.

Take a moment and reflect on your life. Think about your purpose to be God's blessing to the world. How should that change the way you see yourself? How should that change the way you live? Journal your thoughts.

After a few minutes of quiet reflection, continue on to the next station. This will involve your traveling outdoors to an area with a bridge. Make sure everyone has their bags containing the necessary supplies listed for the journey. You may keep this handout.

ISRAEL'S JOURNEY
Station 2
Slavery

Stop at the area designated as "The Promised Land" before crossing the bridge.

READER 1:

The descendants of Abraham were chosen to show the world what it means to live for God and extend God's blessing to the entire earth. God gave Abraham a beautiful land to live in. The land of Canaan was now called The Promised Land, and it was full of rolling hills and the best soil for farming and raising cattle.

But not everything was perfect. They'd soon be known as the people of Israel, or the Israelites, named after Abraham's grandson—a name that means "one who struggles with God."

A few generations after Abraham, a horrible famine swept across the Promised Land, where the Israelites lived. In order to escape this devastating crisis, they packed up their belongings and moved to Egypt.

To symbolize this, we're going to cross the bridge, moving away from the safety of the Promised Land and into a land of great struggle.

Now cross the bridge to the area on the other side, which you've designated as "Slavery, Wandering, & Exile."

READER 2:

While living in Egypt, the Israelites enjoyed great blessings. They grew from a family into a nation, multiplying so quickly that they began to fill the entire country of Egypt.

As their population grew, the king of Egypt—the Pharaoh—told his people:

"The Israelites have become far too numerous for us. Come, we must deal shrewdly with them or they will become even more numerous and, if war breaks out, will join our enemies, fight against us and leave the country." So they put slave masters over them to oppress them with forced labor. —Exodus 1:9-11a

READER 3:

For many years the Egyptians controlled the Israelites as their slaves and treated them terribly.

> But the more [the Israelites] were oppressed, the more they multiplied and spread; so the Egyptians came to dread the Israelites and worked them ruthlessly. They made their lives bitter with harsh labor in brick and mortar and with all kinds of work in the fields; in all their harsh labor the Egyptians used them ruthlessly. —Exodus 1:12-14

> The Israelites groaned in their slavery and cried out, and their cry for help because of their slavery went up to God. God heard their groaning and he remembered his covenant with Abraham, with Isaac and with Jacob. So God looked on the Israelites and was concerned about them. —Exodus 2:23b-25

Have the group members take out their pieces of sour candy or fruit.

Now we'll eat something sour to remind us of how bitter the Israelites' lives were as slaves in Egypt. They were able to withstand the pain of slavery because they put their hope in God.

Quietly sit for a moment with the bitter taste in your mouth. This may burn your mouth a little—reminding you of the pain, struggle, and tears that life can bring.

Have the group members take out their bottles of water.

READER 4:

Now take a drink of water. As the water soothes your throat, remember that God washes over you with care and compassion.

> The Sovereign LORD will wipe away all tears. He will remove forever all insults and mockery against his land and people. —Isaiah 25:8 (NLT)

*HANDOUTS

Praise be to the God and Father of our Lord Jesus Christ, the Father of compassion and the God of all comfort, who comforts us in all our troubles, so that we can comfort those in any trouble with the comfort we ourselves receive from God. For just as we share abundantly in the sufferings of Christ, so also our comfort abounds through Christ. —2 Corinthians 1:3-5

EVERYONE PRAY OUT LOUD

God, you care for me in my pain. In my hardest times, you continue to give me new life and hope. Thank you for never leaving me. Amen.

As a group, walk a ways and find a spot close to the water. Don't cross the bridge back to "The Promised Land." You may keep this handout.

3

ISRAEL'S JOURNEY
Station 3
Exodus

READER 1:

"Therefore, say to the Israelites: 'I am the LORD, and I will bring you out from under the yoke of the Egyptians. I will free you from being slaves to them, and I will redeem you with an outstretched arm and with mighty acts of judgment. I will take you as my own people, and I will be your God. Then you will know that I am the LORD your God, who brought you out from under the yoke of the Egyptians.'" —Exodus 6:6-7

Now we're going to retell the most important story of the Hebrew people—the Exodus. *Exodus* means "to exit," as this story details how the Israelites were set free from hundreds of years of slavery and left Egypt.

As this story is told, picture the events unfolding in your mind like a movie…imagine them coming to life right before you.

READER 2 (based on Exodus 1–15):

God inspired a man named Moses to help rescue the Israelites from slavery. He sent Moses to warn Pharaoh that terrible things would happen to the Egyptians if they didn't release the Israelites.

In his stubbornness Pharaoh said, "Why should I listen to your god? You're trying to create a distraction—stop being lazy and get back to work!"

After this meeting, Pharaoh forced the Israelites to work faster and longer hours. Cruel slave masters pushed them harder and harder to make bricks from mud and straw.

READER 3:

Pharaoh wasn't listening, so God sent a series of warnings, called plagues.

The Nile River turned into blood; the nation was filled with frogs, gnats, and flies; all of the Egyptians' livestock died; people were covered in boils; hail and locusts destroyed the land; and then the sky turned dark for three days.

Many of these elements—the sun, crops, the Nile, cattle, and even frogs—were sacred objects of worship to the Egyptians.

READER 4:

In spite of these horrific events, Pharaoh was stubborn and still wouldn't let the Israelites go.

So God sent one final plague…a plague that would take the life of every firstborn male in Egypt.

But God provided a way for the firstborn of Israel to be spared. The Israelites carefully followed God's instructions to put the blood of a pure sacrificed lamb on the doorframes of their houses.

At midnight, God came through Egypt and took the life of every firstborn son…but passed over the homes with blood on the doorframes. Loud weeping woke everyone during the night. In nearly every Egyptian home someone had died, including Pharaoh's own son. The Egyptians begged the Israelites to leave right away.

READER 1:

Now numbering over two million, the Israelites set out to return to their Promised Land. God guided them through the wilderness with a pillar of fire at night and a pillar of clouds during the day.

When the people of Israel arrived at the banks of a wide sea, they spotted Pharaoh and his armies coming after them in the distance.

Trapped, the Israelites began to panic, screaming at Moses, "Why did you lead us all the way out here to die?"

But Moses reassured the people, "Don't be afraid—God will fight for you and rescue you today!"

Then God told Moses to stretch out his hand over the sea. As he did this, God brought huge winds that opened up a path in the sea for them to walk across!

READER 2:

Soon, Pharaoh and his armies arrived at the banks of the sea and began to follow behind the Israelites on this dry path.

When all of the Israelites arrived safely on the other side of the sea, God told Moses to stretch out his hand again. This brought another huge wind, blowing the waters back over Pharaoh and his armies, completely destroying them!

The people of Israel watched in amazement…in awe of God's power. They danced, sang songs, and celebrated how God had rescued them. The Israelites put their trust in God and in his servant Moses.

This was a day that the people of Israel would celebrate forever![20]

READER 3:

This amazing story has a lot to teach us. One reminder is that we, too, find ourselves in slavery. We may not endure physical slavery, but we experience the real pain and consequences that come from living our own way instead of God's way. Our selfishness and rebellion capture and control us—choking out the life that God intends for us.

The good news is that the story of the exodus is a story of freedom. Just as the Israelites were freed from their Egyptian slavery, God brings freedom to us in our captivity.

For he has rescued us from the dominion of darkness and brought us into the kingdom of the Son he loves, in whom we have redemption, the forgiveness of sins. —Colossians 1:13-14

EVERYONE READ SILENTLY

(Read quietly to yourself)

You've been carrying around a large rock with you today. This weight represents the weight of slavery from which you've been set free.

Take the large rock out of your bag and place your hands on it. Ask God to forgive your selfishness and rebellion and set you free from the things that weigh you down.

Story excerpted from "The Exodus" narrative, based on Exodus 1–15, by Michael Novelli, 2008 (w.echothestory.com).

ISRAEL'S JOURNEY 91

*HANDOUTS

"Come to me, all you who are weary and burdened, and I will give you rest. Take my yoke upon you and learn from me, for I am gentle and humble in heart, and you will find rest for your souls. For my yoke is easy and my burden is light." —Matthew 11:28-30

Thank God for removing your burdens and, as you do, throw your large rock into the water.

Water is where the people of Israel found liberation from their slavery. This symbolizes you leaving behind your old way of life and committing to live a new way—God's way.

When everyone is done praying on their own, walk a few blocks away from the water. Don't cross the bridge to "The Promised Land" yet! You may keep this handout.

4 ISRAEL'S JOURNEY
Station 4
Complaining

DISCUSS

- Are you feeling lighter?

- Who's hungry?

- What's the longest you've ever gone without eating?

- When was it, and why did it happen?

- How did you feel when you finally got food?

READER 1:

It wasn't long after the Israelites left Egypt that they began complaining to Moses. They complained about not having enough to eat and not having water to drink.

> "If only the LORD had killed us back in Egypt," they moaned. "There we sat around pots filled with meat and ate all the bread we wanted. But now you have brought us into this wilderness to starve us all to death." —Exodus 16:3 (NLT)

> Moses cried out in prayer to GOD, "What can I do with these people? Any minute now they'll kill me!" —Exodus 17:4 (*The Message*)

> Then the LORD said to Moses, "Look, I'm going to rain down food from heaven for you. Each day the people can go out and pick up as much food as they need for that day." —Exodus 16:4a (NLT)

So each time the Israelites ran out of food or water, God miraculously provided for them. God sent birds, called quail, to their camp for them to eat; God covered the ground with a sweet, flaky bread-like food; and God even made water pour out of a rock for them to drink!

*HANDOUTS

DISCUSS

- Why were the Israelites complaining? Do you think they had a good reason to complain?

- What did God provide for them?

- How would you have reacted to what God provided?

- In what ways do you struggle with complaining? What do you typically complain about?

- Why do you think people complain so much?

READER 2:

You may now take the sweet treat out of your bag and eat it.

The Bible calls the sweet, flaky food that God provided "manna," which literally means, "What is it?" This mystery food is said to have tasted like honey cakes or doughnuts. Yum! God hadn't forgotten about the Israelites, just as God never forgets about us.

The sweetness of our treat reminds us of the sweetness that God brings—caring for us and providing for us even in difficult times.

> **You have turned my mourning into joyful dancing...and clothed me with joy! —Psalm 30:11 (NLT)**

> **And my God will meet all your needs according to the riches of his glory in Christ Jesus. —Philippians 4:19**

SHARING

Everyone in your group will now share two things for which they're grateful to God.

After your sharing time, walk about one block to an open area. Don't cross the bridge to "The Promised Land" yet! You may keep this handout.

ISRAEL'S JOURNEY
Station 5
Rhythm of Life

READER 1:

Imagine you're one of the people of Israel, standing at the base of a large mountain. Close your eyes as we read this next part of the story.

> Exactly two months after the Israelites left Egypt, they arrived in the wilderness of Sinai...and set up camp there at the base of Mount Sinai.

> On the morning of the third day, thunder roared and lightning flashed, and a dense cloud came down on the mountain. There was a long, loud blast from a ram's horn, and all the people trembled. Moses led them out from the camp to meet with God, and they stood at the foot of the mountain.

> Then God gave the people all these instructions: "I am the LORD your God, who rescued you from the land of Egypt, the place of your slavery." —Exodus 19:1-2, 16-17; 20:1-2 (NLT)

READER 2:

> "You must not have any other god but me. You must not make for yourself an idol of any kind or an image of anything in the heavens or on the earth or in the sea.

> You must not bow down to them or worship them, for I, the LORD your God, am a jealous God who will not tolerate your affection for any other gods. I lay the sins of the parents upon their children; the entire family is affected—even children in the third and fourth generations of those who reject me. But I lavish unfailing love for a thousand generations on those who love me and obey my commands. You must not misuse the name of the LORD your God. The LORD will not let you go unpunished if you misuse his name. Remember to observe the Sabbath day by keeping it holy.

> Honor your father and mother. Then you will live a long, full life in the land the LORD your God is giving you.

*HANDOUTS

> You must not murder.
> You must not commit adultery.
> You must not steal.
> You must not testify falsely against your neighbor.
> You must not covet your neighbor's house. You must not covet your neighbor's wife…or anything else that belongs to your neighbor." —Exodus 20:3-8, 12-17 (NLT)

READER 3:

> When the people heard the thunder and the loud blast of the ram's horn, and when they saw the flashes of lightning and the smoke billowing from the mountain, they stood at a distance, trembling with fear.

> And they said to Moses, "You speak to us, and we will listen. But don't let God speak directly to us, or we will die!"

> "Don't be afraid," Moses answered them, "for God has come in this way to test you, and so that your fear of him will keep you from sinning!"

> As the people stood in the distance, Moses approached the dark cloud where God was. —Exodus 20:18-21 (NLT)

READER 4:

Up on the mountain, God gave Moses more instructions, called laws, to give to Israel. These laws gave specific details about things like how to treat neighbors and enemies, how to handle conflicts, what is fair punishment, when to work and rest, when to celebrate and worship, and what offerings are acceptable to God.

> Then, God gave Moses two stone tablets. On these tablets were the details of the covenant, written by God's finger!

DISCUSS

- What did you picture in your minds as you listened to this story? What stood out to you?
- Why do you think the Israelites needed these commands and laws? Do we need them?

- How do you think God desires for them to be set apart as "royal priests"?
- What might that mean for us?

READER 5:

The Hebrews were God's special people, called to live out God's purposes in the world. The laws and commands weren't meant to be controlling but to give healthy boundaries that provided freedom and protection.

God was trying to help them live in the best possible way—in step with God's design and intentions…in God's rhythm of life. God desires for all humans to experience what the first humans had: *Shalom*—wholeness and completeness found in God.

> Hear, O Israel: The LORD our God, the LORD is one. Love the LORD your God with all your heart and with all your soul and with all your strength. These commandments that I give you today are to be on your hearts. Impress them on your children. Talk about them when you sit at home and when you walk along the road, when you lie down and when you get up. Tie them as symbols on your hands and bind them on your foreheads. Write them on the doorframes of your houses and on your gates. —Deuteronomy 6:4-9

READER 1:

These verses serve as the most important prayer for Jewish people, a prayer they call the *Shema* (pronounced shem-ma), meaning "listen." This prayer is some of the first words a Jewish child will learn and then recite at least twice daily in prayer. Jesus also addressed the importance of the *Shema*:

> One of the teachers of the law came and heard them debating. Noticing that Jesus had given them a good answer, he asked him, "Of all the commandments, which is the most important?"
>
> "The most important one," answered Jesus, "is this: 'Hear, O Israel: The Lord our God, the Lord is one. Love the Lord your God with all your heart and with all your soul and with all your mind and with all your strength.' The second is this: 'Love your neighbor as yourself.' There is no commandment greater than these." —Mark 12:28-31

*HANDOUTS

READER 2:

Not only did Jesus point people to the *Shema*, but he also reminded the Jewish people that loving God also means loving others—these commands are inseparable.

> **"Do not seek revenge or bear a grudge against anyone among your people, but love your neighbor as yourself. I am the LORD." —Leviticus 19:18**

Jesus reaffirmed that the rhythm of all of God's commands and laws are this: Love God and love others.

For an in-depth look at how Jesus reframed the *Shema*, read Scot McKnight's groundbreaking book *The Jesus Creed*.

DISCUSS

- What rhythms or routines do you have in your life?
- What do you think it means to live in God's rhythm of life?
- How do we stand out if we live this way?

READER 3:

The ancient Hebrew people were very hands-on, visual people. Symbols that they could see, taste, and touch were very important to them. They came up with all kinds of ways to remind themselves of the importance of God's commands each day. And many of these activities are still practiced by Jewish people today.

Some of their practices include hanging boxes containing tiny Scripture scrolls (called "phylacteries") from their foreheads and arms to remind them to pray or from the doorframes of their homes (called "mezuzahs") for spiritual and physical protection. They also wore prayer shawls ("tallits") with tassels (or "tzitzit") that reminded them of God's laws. These physical objects are reminders to be attentive to God's way of life at all times.

READER 4:

> **"The days are coming, declares the Lord, when I will make a new covenant...I will put my laws in their minds and write them on their hearts. I will be their God, and they will be my people." —Hebrews 8:8,10**

*HANDOUTS

To provide each of us with a visual reminder of God's rhythm of life, we're going to take out a dry erase marker (not the Sharpie) and ask a friend to write these four words on our left wrists: LOVE GOD, LOVE OTHERS. Be sure to put the dry erase markers back in your bags when you're finished.

DISCUSS

- How could we remind ourselves to live in God's rhythm of life?

- What do you think it means to have the laws (commands) written on your mind and heart?

- How does God's Spirit do this?

GOOD TIP

One way to be reminded of God's rhythms of life is to get a Bible verse sent to you each day. There are a growing number of organizations that send daily Bible verses via text message. Two that look interesting are www.bibletextmessage.com and www.thedailybibleverse.org.

After your group has finished their discussion, you all should walk about 50 steps away from where you are now and away from the bridge. Remember: Don't cross the bridge to "The Promised Land" yet! You may keep this handout.

*HANDOUTS

6 ISRAEL'S JOURNEY
Station 6
Idols

READER 1:

When the people saw how long it was taking Moses to come back down the mountain, they gathered around Aaron [Moses' brother]. "Come on," they said, "make us some gods who can lead us. We don't know what happened to this fellow Moses, who brought us here from the land of Egypt."

So Aaron said, "Take the gold rings from the ears of your wives and sons and daughters, and bring them to me."

All the people took the gold rings from their ears and brought them to Aaron. Then Aaron took the gold, melted it down, and molded it into the shape of a calf. When the people saw it, they exclaimed, "O Israel, these are the gods who brought you out of the land of Egypt!"

Aaron saw how excited the people were, so he built an altar in front of the calf...After this, [the people] celebrated with feasting and drinking, and they indulged in pagan revelry. —Exodus 32:1-5a, 6b (NLT)

READER 2:

Then the LORD said, "I have seen how stubborn and rebellious these people are. Now leave me alone so my fierce anger can blaze against them, and I will destroy them. Then I will make you, Moses, into a great nation."

But Moses tried to pacify the LORD his God. "O LORD!" he said..."Turn away from your fierce anger. Change your mind about this terrible disaster you have threatened against your people!"

So the Lord changed his mind about the terrible disaster he had threatened to bring on his people.

When [Joshua and Moses] came near the camp, Moses saw the calf and the dancing, and he burned with anger. He threw the stone tablets to the ground, smashing them at the foot of the mountain. He took the calf they had made and burned it. Then he ground it into powder, threw it into the water, and forced the people to drink it.

Moses saw that Aaron had let the people get completely out of control, much to the amusement of their enemies. —Exodus 32:9-11a, 12b, 14, 19-20, 25 (NLT)

DISCUSS

- Why do you think the Israelites made an idol to worship?

- Why was it so terrible for them to worship an idol?

- What does this story show us about God?

- What idols do we worship in our culture?

EVERYONE READ SILENTLY

Inside your bag you'll find a small chunk of clay. For the next three minutes, try to sculpt the clay into the shape of something you tend to idolize or put before God.

Now, get into groups of three and share what you created. Then pray for each other, asking for strength to put God first in your lives. As you pray, carefully squeeze your clay idol in your hands, destroying it. After you're done praying, you can use the wipes to clean your hands.

When all of the groups are finished praying, start walking together. Walk about four to six blocks away from where you are—and away from the bridge. Discard your clay in the next trash bin you find. You may keep this handout.

ISRAEL'S JOURNEY
Station 7
Wandering

READER 1:

The people of Israel continued on their journey to the Promised Land. And God gave them a new set of tablets to help them live the right way. During one of Moses' trips up the mountain, God also gave Moses specific instructions about how to build a sacred tent called the Tabernacle.

"Have them make a sanctuary for me, and I will dwell among them." —Exodus 25:8

So Moses gathered the very best craftsmen and workers to build the Tabernacle in the center of the camp. When God was present in this tent, a cloud appeared around it:

Now whenever the cloud lifted from the Tabernacle, the people of Israel would set out on their journey, following it. But if the cloud did not rise, they remained where they were until it lifted. The cloud of the Lord hovered over the Tabernacle during the day, and at night fire glowed inside the cloud so the whole family of Israel could see it. This continued throughout all their journeys. —Exodus 40:36-38 (NLT)

Each day, God guided them through the desert with a cloud, sheltering them from the sun's scorching heat. During the cold desert nights, God guided them with a pillar of fire, providing warmth and light for their journey back to the Promised Land.

READER 2:

But when the people of Israel got close to the Promised Land of Canaan—within a few miles of the border—they wouldn't enter the land because they were afraid of the people who lived there.

"We can't attack those people; they are stronger than we are...All the people we saw there are of great size...We seemed like grasshoppers in our own eyes, and we looked the same to them." —Numbers 13:31b, 32b, 33b

God had promised to fight for them and give them this land, but the Israelites didn't trust God. So God punished them by making them wander in the desert for 40 years. This was a time filled with struggle and complaints against Moses and God.

READER 3:

Right now we're going to walk back toward the bridge, which represents the edge of the Promised Land. We'll gather again there before crossing.

As we walk, pair up with someone and discuss what it must have been like to be an Israelite... wandering in the desert for so long, but also seeing God do amazing things right in front of you.

DISCUSS (AS YOU WALK...)

- What do you think it would have been like to wander in the desert for 40 years?

- What would have been your biggest struggle while wandering?

- Why were the Israelites afraid to enter the Promised Land?

- How do you relate to the Israelites? How are you (we) like them?

- Was there ever a time in your life when you felt like you were wandering or lost? What did you learn from that time?

Walk to the edge of the bridge. When you arrive, stop before crossing over. You may keep this handout.

*HANDOUTS

8 ISRAEL'S JOURNEY
Station 8
Entering into the Promised Land

READER 1:

As Moses neared the end of his life, he reminded the people of Israel about all of God's promises, laws, and commandments. And then he challenged them:

> "Now choose life, so that you and your children may live and that you may love the LORD your God, listen to his voice, and hold fast to him. For the LORD is your life, and he will give you many years in the land he swore to give to your fathers, Abraham, Isaac and Jacob."

> Then Moses summoned Joshua and said to him in the presence of all Israel, "Be strong and courageous, for you must go with this people into the land that the LORD swore to their ancestors to give them, and you must divide it among them as their inheritance. The LORD himself goes before you and will be with you; he will never leave you nor forsake you. Do not be afraid; do not be discouraged." —Deuteronomy 30:19b-20; 31:7-8

After Moses died, Joshua became the new leader of Israel and led them to recapture the Promised Land from their enemies. Finally, after many generations, the people of Israel were able to live in the land God had promised to them.

Right now, as a physical act of our faith, we're going to join hands and cross into the Promised Land. As we do this, ask God to take you to a new place in life, strengthening your faith and trust in God.

Cross the bridge into "The Promised Land."

READER 2:

As the Israelites entered the Promised Land, God performed another miracle for them: God stopped the overflowing Jordan River so they could cross safely on dry ground.

ISRAEL'S JOURNEY Station 8: Entering into the Promised Land

To remember this amazing act, the Israelites built a monument to God, using 12 stones from the middle of the riverbed (one stone for each of Israel's tribes). This monument would serve as a reminder to future generations of how powerful and awesome God is.

Take out the smooth stone and Sharpie marker from your bag. On the stone, write some words that you feel describe God the best. Write as much as you can fit onto the stone! Also put your initials on the rock. After a few minutes, we'll stack our stones and pray together.

Stack your stones as a remembrance of God's faithfulness in your lives. Spend some time praying as a group, asking God to give you faith to live as God's people and set apart to show the world what it means to live in God's ways. After your prayer time, walk to a large open area on the same side of the bridge as "The Promised Land." You may keep this handout.

*HANDOUTS

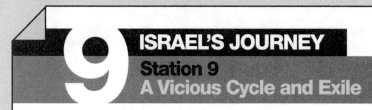

9 ISRAEL'S JOURNEY
Station 9
A Vicious Cycle and Exile

Find a large open area. As a group, walk together in a big circle, then stop where you started.

READER 1:
Finally, the people of Israel were back in their homeland.

> So the LORD gave Israel all the land he had sworn to give their ancestors, and they took possession of it and settled there. The LORD gave them rest on every side, just as he had sworn to their ancestors. Not one of their enemies withstood them; the LORD gave all their enemies into their hands. —Joshua 21:43-44

READER 2:
Things were good, and the Israelites were living in God's ways. Their leader, Joshua, encouraged them to keep on the right path in following God.

> "Be very strong; be careful to obey all that is written in the Book of the Law of Moses, without turning aside to the right or to the left. Do not associate with these nations that remain among you; do not invoke the names of their gods or swear by them. You must not serve them or bow down to them. But you are to hold fast to the LORD your God, as you have until now." —Joshua 23:6-8

DISCUSS

- What do you think happened?

READER 3:
Corrupt people still lived in Canaan—and right next to the Israelites. God had told them to drive these people out of the country, but the Israelites didn't listen.

Just as Joshua warned, the people became enticed by the false gods and destructive ways of the people that remained in the Promised Land. Soon the Israelites forgot about God, and they walked away from living in God's rhythm of life.

All the people did whatever seemed right in their own eyes. —Judges 21:25b (NLT)

READER 4:

Slowly turn your head to the right and to the left. Do this several times. This is what the people of Israel were doing. They were distracted by the culture around them, and they became consumed with living their own way and giving themselves to false gods.

> But the people replied, "Don't waste your breath. We will continue to live as we want to, stubbornly following our own evil desires." —Jeremiah 18:12 (NLT)

Follow the same path of the circle you just walked and walk halfway around the circle together.

READER 5:

Walking away from God also meant walking away from God's protection. While the Israelites were living their own way, bad things began happening to them. They became entangled in conflict and wars—among themselves and with other nations. They were continually being attacked and conquered and forced into slavery once again.

Get on your knees. This position represents a place of surrender in which the Israelites found themselves. As they were defeated, the people of Israel began to suffer, so they begged God for help and forgiveness.

Now open your hands up to God and shout, "Help us, God!" This may seem strange, but this will help you remember and identify with the story.

READER 1:

Out of great concern, God sent help to the Israelites—sometimes through miracles and oftentimes through leaders called "judges" (who'd later be replaced by kings) to lead them in defeating their enemies.

> Whenever the LORD raised up a judge for them, he was with the judge and saved them out of the hands of their enemies as long as the judge lived; for the LORD relented because of their groaning under those who oppressed and afflicted them. —Judges 2:18

So battle after battle, Israel conquered their enemies at every border. In victory, the people would worship God.

"I called to the LORD, who is worthy of praise, and have been saved from my enemies" —2 Samuel 22:4

Get up, join arms with each other, and walk back to where you started the circle.

READER 2:

As you might have guessed, things didn't remain good for the people of Israel.

But when the judge died, the people returned to ways even more corrupt than those of their ancestors, following other gods and serving and worshiping them. They refused to give up their evil practices and stubborn ways. —Judges 2:19

Unfortunately, this became a pattern from generation to generation. The people of Israel would come to God and worship whenever they needed help; but when things were going well, they returned to worshiping other things.

LIFE SEEMS GOOD
no major conflicts, lots to eat,
good health, lots of posessions

TURN TO GOD'S WAYS
praying, seek
forgiveness, live rightly

ANCIENT ISRAEL'S CYCLE

TURN TO OUR WAYS
selfishness, greed,
power, control

LIFE IS NOT GOOD
conflicts, defeat, hunger,
poverty, slavery, pain, suffering

DISCUSS

- Look at the chart showing Israel's Cycle. Are we like the Israelites? What patterns do we get into that aren't good?

- Based on all of the stories we've looked at so far, what do you think God desires from people?

- What do you think it takes to be a part of the faithful remnant?

READER 3:

This was a time filled with struggle and rebellion for Israel. But there were moments of hope—brief periods when a glimpse of God's kingdom could be seen. Under the rule of King David and his son Solomon, people experienced God's presence in the temple—a permanent Tabernacle—and lived in harmony with each other for a time.

But this didn't last long. Solomon, and most of the kings who came after him, turned away from God and relied on false gods. Civil war broke out, splitting the Israelites into two kingdoms: Israel and Judah. Other nations eventually conquered both kingdoms of Israel and destroyed the temple.

The Israelites were forced out of the Promised Land, becoming enslaved or exiled to other countries and taken away from their homes and all that was familiar.

READER 4:

As we travel back to our first location, tell me what you think about this journey we've been on today. What stands out to you?

There is one more station—a bright spot in the story as we turn our attention toward future hope.

Meet in the same room as you did for the first station. You may keep this handout.

10 ISRAEL'S JOURNEY
Station 10
Future Hope

READER 1:

It would seem all hope was lost…but not with God. If the people's appointed leaders wouldn't be faithful, then God would raise up other voices, called "prophets." They'd cry out for justice and for the people to return to God's kingdom ways.

God sent a message of hope through these prophets, promising that a time would come when Israel would be free and united once again. The prophets continued to keep the dream of God's kingdom on earth alive in their hearts.

> **"For I will take you out of the nations; I will gather you from all the countries and bring you back into your own land. I will sprinkle clean water on you, and you will be clean; I will cleanse you from all your impurities and from all your idols. I will give you a new heart and put a new spirit in you; I will remove from you your heart of stone and give you a heart of flesh. And I will put my Spirit in you and move you to follow my decrees and be careful to keep my laws. Then you will live in the land I gave your ancestors; you will be my people, and I will be your God." —Ezekiel 36:24-28**

READER 2:

God fulfills the promises, and after 70 years the Israelites return to rebuild and repopulate their land. This was a bittersweet reunion, as many of the Israelites remembered what they'd lost.

Through these prophets, God promised to send someone to rescue them from their rebellion and the oppression of other nations. This would be a new kind of king—a Messiah who would bring about God's kingdom in fullness and rule forever.

God gave the prophets visions of what this Messiah would be like.

TAKE TURNS READING: (verses are paraphrased)

> **He will be a descendant of King David. —2 Samuel 7:16, Isaiah 9:7**

ISRAEL'S JOURNEY Station 10: Future Hope

A messenger from the wilderness will challenge people to prepare for his coming. —Isaiah 40:3

A virgin will give birth to him in Bethlehem, and he will be called Immanuel. —Isaiah 7:14, Micah 5:2

God's Spirit will be upon him and he will bring justice. —Isaiah 11:2; 42:1

He will begin his ministry in Galilee. —Isaiah 9:1

He will bring good news and healing to the poor, brokenhearted, and sick. —Isaiah 61:1-3

He will set captives free and open the eyes of the blind. —Isaiah 42:7

He will do no wrong, living a life without rebellion. —Isaiah 53:9

He will be a light to guide the nations—reaching people all over the world. —Isaiah 42:6

He will be called Wonderful Counselor, Mighty God, Everlasting Father, Prince of Peace. —Isaiah 9:6

He will be despised, forgotten, and rejected by his own people. —Isaiah 53:3

He will be beaten, whipped, and wounded—all so we can have peace, healing, and forgiveness. —Isaiah 53:5-6

He will be silent when faced with accusations. He will be put on trial and thrown in prison. —Isaiah 53:7

He will be killed like a criminal and buried in a rich man's tomb. —Isaiah 53:9

God will lay the punishment and guilt for all of our sins on him. His life will be made an offering for us. —Isaiah 53:5-6,10-12

Because of him, many will be made right with God. —Isaiah 53:11

His kingdom will rule with peace and justice forever. —Isaiah 9:7

*HANDOUTS

READER 3:

As we close our time together, let's focus on the hope that was found in the true Messiah, Jesus.

> "I, the LORD, have called you to demonstrate my righteousness. I will take you by the hand and guard you, and I will give you to my people, Israel, as a symbol of my covenant with them. *And you will be a light to guide the nations.*" —Isaiah 42:6 (NLT) (emphasis added)

One of the most important symbols for the Jewish people is a *menorah*, which means "lampstand." The first menorah was built for the Tabernacle and had seven candles connected to the same base. The menorah was the only light in the Tabernacle, and the priests kept it lit 24 hours a day. This special light was a reminder of God's continual presence and watch over us.

We will light these seven candles now, symbolizing the light of Jesus the Messiah pushing away the darkness in our lives.

EVERYONE PRAY OUT LOUD

God,

We are grateful to learn more about the people of Israel.

We're like our spiritual ancestors in so many ways,

struggling to find ourselves apart from you.

May you draw us back in to your rhythms today.

Thank you for being our light.

May you shine in us and through us,

helping us to live in your ways,

and bring hope and healing to a hurting world.

Amen.

You may keep this handout.

THE TABERNACLE

DEVELOPED BY MICHAEL NOVELLI
WITH SETH MCCOY

*INSTRUCTIONS

DESCRIPTION

Participants will enter the Tabernacle to learn more about the customs and rituals of the Israelites and reflect on what this might mean for their own lives. Handouts will guide participants to interact with objects from the Tabernacle at each station and connect some of the symbols to Jesus.

LOCATIONS AND LOGISTICS

- There are 10 stations—each one takes about six minutes to complete with time to move between stations. The journey should take about 75 minutes altogether.

- It will take four or five people to run this experience. It should be fairly simple to set up, depending on how much prep work there is to get the spaces ready. Unless you have an outdoor tent, stations should be set up in an open room. These stations should take about five to ten minutes each to set up.

- One staff facilitator is needed for every two stations (although Station 10 doesn't need any adult support), and instructions are provided for each facilitator. One of the most important roles of the facilitator is to gently keep the groups moving through the experience on schedule. After a group leaves a station, the facilitator will reset the station, if necessary, and cue the next group.

- Create a reflective atmosphere in the room—make it dimly lit with candles, play some gentle background music, and soften up the space by hanging large pieces of fabric around the room. This will help participants get a sense that this is a special place.

GROUP SIZE

People should enter in groups of six to eight, including an adult leader. If you'd like, all of the groups can meet up and talk about their experience at the last station.

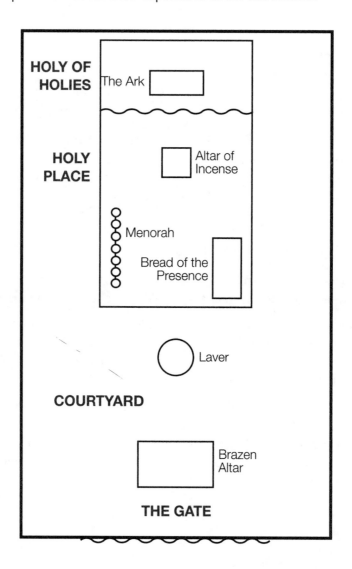

STATIONS (STOPPING POINTS)

STATION 1: LIVING AROUND THE TABERNACLE

LOCATION AND PREPARATION

This will be a basic description of the function and appearance of the Tabernacle. Centered in this station will be an enlarged color illustration of the Tabernacle that participants will sit around to observe writing down their thoughts and reactions to it. This illustration could be printed and displayed or projected onto a screen or bed sheet.

MATERIALS

- Tabernacle illustration (purchase a print of this image at http://www.selahart.com).
- A video projector with computer hookup.
- A screen or large white sheet on which to project the image.
- If using a print of the illustration, you'll need a short easel and a desk lamp to display and illuminate the illustration.
- A candle or small light for the reader to use and to gently illuminate the room.
- 10 copies of the Station 1 handouts—returned by participants (available on accompanying CD).

Tabernacle Illustration

STATION 2: THE GATE

LOCATION AND PREPARATION

Participants will enter the station and face the gate: A curtain hung with either portable pipes and drapes or curtain rods and poles. At the end of this station, they'll walk through this gate to move further into their experience with God.

MATERIALS

- A pair of 7 ft. upright posts that can support a curtain rod for participants to walk underneath. (A suggestion: If you don't have pipe and drape, take two five-gallon buckets and center a seven-foot-tall two-by-four into each one. Mix some Quikrete to fill the buckets and let dry. Screws could then be run into the tops of the pieces of wood to hold a normal curtain rod.)
- Two dark-colored curtains or drapes (hanging on a rod connected to the uprights at each end) with a split in the center so people can walk through.
- A candle or small light for the reader to use and to gently illuminate the room.
- 10 copies of the Station 2 handouts—returned by participants (available on accompanying CD).

STATION 3: BRAZEN ALTAR

LOCATION AND PREPARATION

The altar for sacrificing animals was the first thing a person saw when entering the Tabernacle. Place large pieces of butcher paper or art paper on a table with bowls of thick, red or brown paint. Participants will put their palms into the paint, make prints on the paper, and think about having blood on their hands. They'll move on from this station with dirty hands.

MATERIALS

- A large table for eight people to gather around.
- Shallow plates or trays (large enough to fit at least one hand, if not both) to hold paint.
- A roll of butcher paper or 3M large Post-it sheets.
- A drop cloth for under the table.

- A candle or small light for the reader to use and to gently illuminate the room.
- 10 copies of the Station 3 handouts—returned by participants (available on accompanying CD).

STATION 4: LAVER
LOCATION AND PREPARATION

The laver immediately followed the altar so that dirty hands and feet could be washed and cleansed. Dirty hands will be placed in bowls of clean water. While their hands are coming clean, participants will pray and reflect on the cross and their new purity before God.

MATERIALS

- Eight large bowls arranged in a half circle around the station.
- Plenty of five-gallon buckets full of clean water for refilling.
- Plenty of five-gallon buckets to hold the dirty water after rinsing.
- Plenty of paper towels.
- Trash bags for dirty paper towels.
- A candle or small light for the reader to use and to gently illuminate the room,
- 10 copies of the Station 4 handouts—returned by participants (available on accompanying CD).

STATION 5: MENORAH (LAMPSTAND)
LOCATION AND PREPARATION

The menorah was the source of light for the Holy Place and was a representation of Israel as a light to the nations. Participants will observe the flames and reflect on their lives and their groups. Participants will listen for anything the Holy Spirit may want to illuminate to them and then journal their thoughts.

MATERIALS

- A menorah with oil, wicks, and stand or seven candles large enough to burn for a few hours without melting out.

- A table on which to place the menorah or candles.

- 10 copies of the Station 5 handouts—returned by participants (available on accompanying CD).

STATION 6: BREAD OF THE PRESENCE

LOCATION AND PREPARATION

On this table are 12 loaves of bread representing the 12 tribes of Israel. At the center of this room is a table small enough for the groups to sit around and eat. They'll pass the bread and tear off pieces as they pray for each other and for their youth group's unity.

MATERIALS

- A small table to hold 12 pieces of pita bread in two stacks of six.

- Table must be a height where people can sit around it and see each other.

- Enough bread to replenish as the groups go through.

- A candle or small light for the reader to use and to gently illuminate the room.

- 10 copies of the Station 6 handouts—returned by participants (available on accompanying CD).

STATION 7: ALTAR OF INCENSE

LOCATION AND PREPARATION

The incense in this room is both a visual and scent-related object. As the smoke rises, participants will think about their worries, anxieties, and fears and let them rise to God as prayers. As they smell the scent, they'll also pray for their group.

MATERIALS

- A small table to hold the incense.

- A strong but pleasant-smelling incense that's large enough to give off a visible plume and to last for the whole experience.

- A candle or small light for the reader to use and to gently illuminate the room.

- 10 copies of the Station 7 handouts—returned by participants (available on accompanying CD).

Note: *Be careful! Before you strike a match, check with the powers that be on any fire-code restrictions involving incense or candles.*

STATION 8: THE HOLY OF HOLIES AND THE VEIL

LOCATION AND PREPARATION

The veil will be in the center of the room, like the gate. On the other side of the veil will be a candle, representing God's presence, and a rope coming out from under the veil. Participants will observe the veil and journal about how it would feel to be separated from God. They will then walk to the other side and sit down around the candle, symbolizing that they can now be with God.

MATERIALS

- A pair of 7 ft. upright posts that can support a curtain rod for participants to walk underneath (See suggestions from Station Two).

- Two dark-colored curtains or drapes (hanging on a rod connected to the uprights at each end) with a split in the center so people can walk through.

- A rope to run out from under the veil.

- A large three-wick candle sitting on the floor to represent God's presence.

- A candle or small light for the reader to use and to gently illuminate the room.

- 10 copies of the Station 8 handouts—returned by participants (available on accompanying CD).

STATION 9: THE ARK OF THE COVENANT AND THE MERCY SEAT

LOCATION AND PREPARATION

The ark contained three articles that the participants will explore and journal about. The bread, stick, and stones will serve as representatives of the manna, Aaron's budding staff, and the stone tablets containing the Ten Commandments. Participants will reflect and journal on their own patterns of unfaithfulness. The group will take a white sheet and place it over these items, signifying the covering over of their unfaithfulness by the atonement of Jesus. The group will also write their names on a helium-filled balloon that they'll take with them to the last station.

MATERIALS

- A clear jar containing bread (preferably the same type of bread used in Station 6).
- A large stick the size of a walking stick or staff.
- Two medium-sized stones (the size of a cantaloupe).
- A table that can hold all of these items—such as a coffee table.
- A white sheet.
- Red helium-filled balloons with strings—one for each group (but make sure you have extras).
- 10 Sharpie markers.
- 10 copies of the Station 9 handouts—returned by participants (available on accompanying CD).

STATION 10: THE RELEASE AND GROUP INTERACTION

LOCATION AND PREPARATION

The group will head outside to pray over and release their balloons, which symbolize God taking away their sin. Groups will also gather for dialogue and discussion.

- 10 copies of the Station 10 handouts—returned by participants (available on accompanying CD).

THE TABERNACLE
Introduction

EVERYONE READ SILENTLY

This is an important time to…

- Connect with God and
- Connect with others in meaningful ways.

This time requires you to…

- Slow down and turn off your cell phone.
- Enter into a different pace of life.
- Speak quietly and act respectfully.
- Think deeply and engage your mind and heart.
- Be open to what God has for you.

We hope that through this experience you'll see how your story is connected to and a continuation of a bigger Story that began thousands of years ago.

Pray quietly and ask God to help you enter the story.

You will enter this experience in groups of six to eight people. At each station, different people from your group will read parts aloud. You don't have to read if you don't want to, but as many people as possible should read and help guide the experience.

*HANDOUTS

THE TABERNACLE
Station 1
Living Around the Tabernacle

READER 1:

You're about to begin a walk-through experience of the Tabernacle. *Tabernacle* means "tent," "place of dwelling," or "sanctuary." It was a special place where God chose to meet the Israelites as they wandered in the wilderness, and where the leaders and people came together to worship and offer sacrifices.

Through sight, sound, smell, and touch, you'll get a chance to imagine what the Tabernacle must have been like and to spend time connecting with God in unique ways.

Please leave the handouts in a neat stack for the next group. Now quietly proceed to Station 1 with your group.

READER 2:

God called a special people to show the world what it means to live the best possible way—God's way. These people were called the Israelites, or people of Israel, a name that means "one who struggles with God."

The people of Israel were on a long journey to return home to a place called the Promised Land. God gave their leader, a man named Moses, specific instructions about how to build a sacred meeting place called the Tabernacle.

"Have them make a sanctuary for me, and I will dwell among them." —Exodus 25:8

This portable sanctuary was a tent that God inhabited while they traveled. So Moses gathered the very best craftsmen and workers to build the Tabernacle in the center of their camp. When God was present in this tent, a cloud appeared around it:

Now whenever the cloud lifted from the Tabernacle, the people of Israel would set out on their journey, following it. But if the cloud did not rise, they remained where they were until it lifted. The cloud of the LORD hovered over the Tabernacle during the day, and at night fire glowed inside the cloud so the whole family of Israel could see it. This continued throughout all their journeys. —Exodus 40:36-38 (NLT)

THE TABERNACLE **Station 1:** **Living Around the Tabernacle**

Each day, God guided them through the desert with a cloud, sheltering them from the sun's scorching heat. During the cold desert nights, God guided them with a pillar of fire, providing warmth and light for their journey back to the Promised Land.

DISCUSS

Look at the picture of the Tabernacle. Slow down and look it over carefully. Quietly discuss your observations with your group.

- What catches your eye first?

- What details do you notice?

- What questions do you have?

- The Tabernacle was always set up in the middle of the Israelites' camp. What would it have been like to live near the Tabernacle?

READER 3:

**The Word became flesh and made his dwelling among us. We have seen his glory, the glory of the one and only [Son], who came from the Father, full of grace and truth.
—John 1:14**

The word *dwelling* in this verse is the same word they used for *Tabernacle* in the Old Testament. In other words, God became human in order to dwell or to "Tabernacle" among his people. So as he walked upon the earth and lived among the people of Israel, Jesus fulfilled the picture of the Old Testament Tabernacle.

As you go through this experience today, think about how the elements you encounter can also be symbolic of Jesus.

Please put your handouts in a neat stack for the next group and continue on to the next station.

THE TABERNACLE
Station 2
The Gate

READER 1:

A courtyard measuring 150 feet by 75 feet (smaller than a hockey rink or indoor soccer field) surrounded the Tabernacle. And a seven-foot-high fence made of thick linen strips that were hung on poles enclosed the courtyard. This fabric fence had only one entrance—a 30-foot-wide gate right in the center. The gate was covered with finely woven blue, purple, and scarlet linen.

Each day, people lined up outside the gate to bring their sacrifices to God. The gate was the passageway for the people of Israel to find forgiveness and to be in God's presence.

"You must bring everything I command you—your burnt offerings, your sacrifices, your tithes, your sacred offerings, and your offerings to fulfill a vow—to the designated place of worship, the place the LORD your God chooses for his name to be honored." —Deuteronomy 12:11 (NLT)

READER 2:

Sacrifices and offerings were a common part of most ancient religions. But for the Israelites, God provided boundaries and a deeper meaning for this practice.

Offerings and sacrifices weren't made simply for obtaining forgiveness for wrongdoing. All kinds of offerings were made to God—praise, peace, thankfulness, love, gratitude, celebration, and cleansing.

The Hebrew word for *sacrifice* is *korban*, which means "to come close and draw near." This is a reminder that the primary purpose of offerings and sacrifices was to reconnect with God.

READER 3:

"I am the gate; whoever enters through me will be saved." —John 10:9

Jesus answered, "I am the way and the truth and the life. No one comes to the Father except through me." —John 14:6

THE TABERNACLE Station 2: The Gate

The curtain in front of you represents the Tabernacle gate. Now close your eyes and picture the Tabernacle in your mind.

Imagine yourself standing in front of the gate. What do you feel?

Beyond the gate is an experience with the living God. Think about what it means for you to walk through the gate, finding forgiveness and fellowship with God.

Now take a moment and quietly tell God what you're feeling and thinking. When you're ready, walk through the gate.

After you walk through the gate, please put your handouts in a neat stack for the next group and continue on to the next station—the brazen altar.

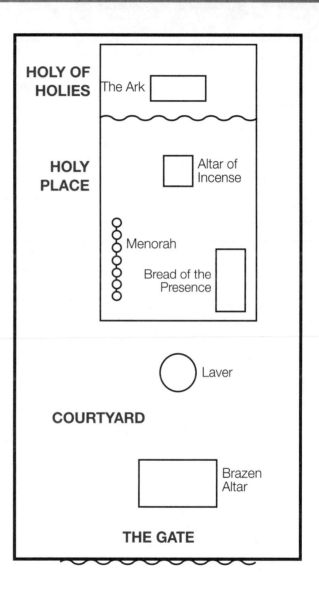

*HANDOUTS

3 THE TABERNACLE
Station 3
Brazen Altar

READER 1:

As the people entered the courtyard, the brazen altar was the first thing they saw. It was a large wooden box (4 1/2 feet high by 7 1/2 feet long) without a lid that was set on top of a mound of earth, making it higher than everything else in the courtyard. Inside the box was a crate for holding live animals.

The Israelites brought animals—males without blemish or defect—to the priest at the brazen altar. The priest then laid his hands on the sacrifice, which symbolized the person's sin and guilt being transferred to the animal.

The LORD called to Moses from the Tabernacle and said to him, "Give the following instructions to the people of Israel. When you present an animal as an offering to the LORD, you may take it from your herd of cattle or your flock of sheep and goats. If the animal you present as a burnt offering is from the herd, it must be a male with no defects. Bring it to the entrance of the Tabernacle so you may be accepted by the LORD. Lay your hand on the animal's head, and the LORD will accept its death in your place to purify you, making you right with him. —Leviticus 1:1-4 (NLT)

READER 2:

The priest slaughtered the animal, sprinkled some of its blood in front of the Tabernacle, burned the sacrifice, and then poured the rest of the blood at the bottom of the altar. The first sacrifices were made in the Tabernacle exactly one year after the first Passover. The animal sacrifices reminded the people of the Passover lambs that were sacrificed in order to save their firstborns from the last plague of God's judgment on Egypt.

To the people of Israel, blood represented the value of life and purity. Each family brought sacrifices year after year. In addition, the priests offered daily sacrifices for the wrongdoings of the entire nation. These offerings in themselves were a symbol—God's forgiveness came only with a sincere heart and a turning away from wrongdoing.

THE TABERNACLE Station 3: Brazen Altar

"If my people, who are called by my name, will humble themselves and pray and seek my face and turn from their wicked ways, then I will hear from heaven, and I will forgive their sin and will heal their land." —2 Chronicles 7:14

READER 3:

In our culture the practice of animal sacrifice may be difficult to relate to. But in the time of the Israelites, most families raised animals and butchered them for food. This was a normal part of life and necessary for the people's survival.

For the Israelites, the most difficult part about the sacrifice would have been the financial loss. The very best animals were required for sacrifice—the biggest and the healthiest. One animal could feed a family for weeks, so making the sacrifice could cost them up to one year's salary.

Through these daily sacrifices, the people of Israel were constantly reminded of God's grace and provision. They understood the importance and symbolism of surrendering a huge part of their livelihood. This sacrifice revealed a heart that was truly dependent on God.

READER 4:

Now close your eyes.

Picture yourself as part of a family whose tent was located close to the Tabernacle. Picture the sounds and smells of sacrifice that rose from the Tabernacle twice a day—once in the morning and once in the evening.

Christ, our Passover Lamb, has been sacrificed for us. —1 Corinthians 5:7b (NLT)

Unlike those other high priests, [Jesus] does not need to offer sacrifices every day. They did this for their own sins first and then for the sins of the people. But Jesus did this once for all when he offered himself as the sacrifice for the people's sins. —Hebrews 7:27 (NLT)

Just as the brazen altar of the Tabernacle was raised on a mound of dirt, so the cross of Jesus was raised on a hill. Jesus became our Passover Lamb and a final sacrifice for all of our wrongdoing. In his

*HANDOUTS

innocence Jesus bore the consequence for all who step outside of God's ways—death. He opened up a way for us to be rescued from our destructive behaviors and join a better way.

THE MARK OF REBELLION

Dip one of your palms into the bowl of paint.

Now take your dirty hand and make a handprint on the paper.

Slow down. Take a minute to look at your hand and think about how it feels to be dirty, to have your life stained by rebellion and selfishness. Think about Jesus' blood shed for you and what it cost him to be your offering to God.

Please put your handouts in a neat stack for the next group and continue on to the next station—with your hand still dirty.

THE TABERNACLE
Station 4
Laver

READER 1:

A bronze water basin, called a *laver*, was centrally located in the courtyard of the Tabernacle. It stood as a reminder for the people that they needed to be clean before they approached God.

Moses' brother, Aaron, and his sons were chosen to represent the people as priests. They had the special job of bringing the people's offerings to God. The priests were required to use this basin to thoroughly wash their hands and feet before entering the Tabernacle. If they entered the presence of God in an impure manner, they'd die.

> Then the LORD said to Moses, "Make a bronze basin, with its bronze stand, for washing. Place it between the tent of meeting and the altar, and put water in it. Aaron and his sons are to wash their hands and feet with water from it. Whenever they enter the tent of meeting, they shall wash with water so that they will not die." —Exodus 30:17-20a

READER 2:

> "Though your sins are like scarlet, they shall be as white as snow; though they are red as crimson, they shall be like wool." —Isaiah 1:18b

Place your hands in a water basin but keep them still. How does the water feel? Silently tell God how you're feeling and spend a moment receiving God's cleansing and forgiveness.

While you're silently praying, slowly wash your hands, making sure to get them thoroughly clean. Then use paper towels to dry your hands.

When your hands are clean and dry, look at them and spend a moment thanking Jesus for making you as clean as freshly fallen snow.

> Let us go right into the presence of God with sincere hearts fully trusting him. For our guilty consciences have been sprinkled with Christ's blood to make us clean, and our bodies have been washed with pure water. —Hebrews 10:22 (NLT)

After everyone has finished cleaning their hands and praying, put your handouts in a neat stack for the next group and continue on to the next station.

*HANDOUTS

THE TABERNACLE
Station 5
Menorah

READER 1:

You're now standing inside the Tabernacle. It was divided into two rooms, and the large outer room was called the Holy Place. In this room was a menorah, or lampstand, that held seven oil lamps. The priests were instructed to keep these lamps burning continuously. The lampstand was the only source of light in the Holy Place. Without it, the priests would have been completely in the dark.

It's been said the menorah is a symbol of the nation of Israel and its mission to be a light to the world—a new kind of people who'd show the world what it means to live in God's ways.

> But you are a chosen people, a royal priesthood, a holy nation, God's special possession, that you may declare the praises of him who called you out of darkness into his wonderful light. —1 Peter 2:9

READER 2:

> So Samuel took the horn of oil and anointed [David] in the presence of his brothers, and from that day on the Spirit of the LORD came on David in power. —1 Samuel 16:13a

The oil used in the Tabernacle's lamps is symbolic of the Holy Spirit. Take a minute to slow down and sense God's Spirit around and in you. Listen for God to bring words of comfort and encouragement to your mind.

> Blessed are those who have learned to acclaim you, who walk in the light of your presence, LORD. —Psalm 89:15

READER 3:

> For you were once darkness, but now you are light in the Lord. Live as children of light (for the fruit of the light consists in all goodness, righteousness and truth). —Ephesians 5:8-9

THE TABERNACLE Station 5: Menorah

Select one flame from the menorah and fix your eyes upon it. Watch it burn for a minute or two.

- As you look at this light, think about your life. Are you bringing light to others? How?

- Are there areas of your life that are causing your flame to grow dim?

- Whisper a prayer to God to make your light shine brighter.

READER 4:

"You are the light of the world. A city on a hill cannot be hidden. Neither do people light a lamp and put it under a bowl. Instead they put it on its stand, and it gives light to everyone in the house. In the same way, let your light shine before others, that they may see your good deeds and glorify your Father in heaven." —Matthew 5:14-16

Look around the room and see how the menorah is spreading light in a dark place. As these flames burn together, they burn brighter than they would alone.

We have the privilege of reflecting the light of Jesus in a world filled with pain, despair, and darkness. How could our group shine light in the community around us?

Join hands and pray that God will shine his light of love through your group. Then put your handouts in a neat stack for the next group and continue on to the next station.

6 THE TABERNACLE
Station 6
Bread of the Presence

Gather around the table and pause for a few seconds of silence.

READER 1:

Inside the Holy Place was a table with 12 loaves of bread separated into two stacks. These 12 loaves symbolized the 12 tribes of Israel. The bread was known as "showbread," or "the bread of the presence," and it was a reminder of God's continual presence and never-failing provision.

> "You must bake twelve loaves of bread from choice flour, using four quarts of flour for each loaf. Place the bread before the LORD on the pure gold table, and arrange the loaves in two rows, with six loaves in each row…Every Sabbath day this bread must be laid out before the LORD. The bread is to be received from the people of Israel as a requirement of the eternal covenant. The loaves of bread will belong to Aaron and his descendants, who must eat them in a sacred place, for they are most holy." —Leviticus 24:5-6, 8-9a (NLT)

Once a week on the Sabbath, the priests ate the bread and then put fresh bread on the table. This bread was considered to be sacred, and only the priests could eat it in the Holy Place.

READER 2:

> Then Jesus declared, "I am the bread of life. Whoever comes to me will never go hungry, and whoever believes in me will never be thirsty." —John 6:35

> "I no longer call you servants, because servants do not know their master's business. Instead, I have called you friends, for everything that I learned from my Father I have made known to you." —John 15:15

Out of great care for humans, God provides all that we need each day. We're invited to sit at God's table as a friend and live in close relationship with God. Jesus provided a way for us to be a part of God's family and enjoy God's blessings.

THE TABERNACLE   Station 6: Bread of the Presence

READER 3:

Every day they continued to meet together in the temple courts. They broke bread in their homes and ate together with glad and sincere hearts, praising God and enjoying the favor of all the people. And the Lord added to their number daily those who were being saved. —Acts 2:46-47

READER 4:

Sharing a meal is an act of friendship. The table and bread reminded the Israelites to live in a close relationship with God and with each other. As we pass this loaf of bread around the table, tear off a piece and hold on to it.

After everyone has a piece of bread, take a moment to look at the people who are sitting around the table. God has given us the privilege of being a family that's united.

Eat the bread together and spend the next few minutes praying for your brothers or sisters who are sitting at the table with you. If you have any differences, plan to resolve them today.

After your prayer time, put your handouts in a neat stack for the next group and continue on to the next station.

THE TABERNACLE
Station 7
Altar of Incense

READER 1:

The altar of incense sat in front of the curtain that separated the Holy Place from the Holy of Holies. This was a small square altar made of wood and pure gold.

> "Aaron must burn fragrant incense on the altar every morning when he tends the lamps. He must burn incense again when he lights the lamps at twilight so incense will burn regularly before the LORD for the generations to come." —Exodus 30:7-8

God instructed the priests to burn incense on this golden altar every morning and evening at the same time the burnt offerings were made. God gave them specific instructions for the mixture of spices and fragrances that was to be burned.

READER 2:

This incense was a symbol of the prayers and intercessions of the people, rising up to God as a sweet fragrance.

> May my prayer be set before you like incense; may the lifting up of my hands be like the evening sacrifice. —Psalms 141:2

Watch the incense rising. Follow it with your eyes as it floats upward.

The Bible says we're to take our anxieties, worries, and fears and reshape them into prayers, letting them rise up to God.

> Do not be anxious about anything, but in every situation, by prayer and petition, with thanksgiving, present your requests to God. And the peace of God, which transcends all understanding, will guard your hearts and your minds in Christ Jesus. —Philippians 4:6-7

THE TABERNACLE Station 7: Altar of Incense

What are your worries, anxieties, and fears? As you think of them, watch the smoke rise and release them to God.

Feel the burden of your anxieties lifted as God's Spirit takes them and comforts you.

Now close your eyes and breathe deeply. Let the smell of the incense soak in.

Just as the smell of this fragrance is pleasing to your senses, so your prayers are pleasing to God.

Our lives are a Christ-like fragrance rising up to God. —2 Corinthians 2:15a (NLT)

Spend the next few minutes praying, and then put your handouts in a neat stack for the next group before continuing on to Station 8.

*HANDOUTS

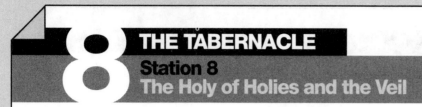

8 THE TABERNACLE
Station 8
The Holy of Holies and the Veil

READER 1:
Inside the Holy Place was another room called the Holy of Holies. This was a sacred room, God's special dwelling place where no ordinary person could enter.

A four-inch thick curtain, known as the veil, hung from the tent ceiling all the way down to the floor, separating the Holy of Holies from the Holy Place. It took hundreds of men to put this curtain in place, as it was 60 feet high and weighed several tons. This curtain was made of fine linen and blue, purple, and scarlet yarn, with figures of angels embroidered onto it.

Whoever entered into the Holy of Holies entered the very presence of God. In fact, if anyone except the high priest entered the Holy of Holies, they'd die. Even the high priest, God's chosen mediator with Israel, could pass through the veil only once a year on a special day called the Day of Atonement.

READER 2:
God told the Israelites this about this special Day of Atonement:

> "Do no work during that entire day because it is the Day of Atonement, when offerings of purification are made for you, making you right with the Lord your God."
> —Leviticus 23:28 (NLT)

God gave the high priest very specific instructions to follow on the Day of Atonement. The high priest had to make sure he was completely clean—both in body and soul. He was also instructed to wear special clothing and an elaborate robe. He wore a breastplate with the names of the 12 tribes of Israel engraved on it, showing that he represented his people before God.

The priest then sacrificed a young bull as payment for his and his family's wrongdoing, dipped his finger in the blood, entered the Holy of Holies, and sprinkled the blood on the cover and the front of the ark of the covenant.

THE TABERNACLE Station 8: The Holy of Holies and the Veil

READER 3:

The priest also found two spotless goats and sacrificed one of them as a substitute for the wrongdoings of all of the Israelites. The blood of this sacrifice was also sprinkled on the ark.

The goat that wasn't sacrificed was called the "scapegoat," or *azazel*, which means, "to take away."

The high priest laid both of his hands on the animal's head and confessed all of the people's wrongdoings for the year. This put them on the head of the goat. Then the goat was led far away into the wilderness, never to be seen again.

The goat will carry on itself all their sins to a remote place; and the man shall release it in the wilderness. —Leviticus 16:22

If these things were not done exactly as God prescribed, the high priest would die. Since no one else could enter the Holy of Holies, the other priests tied bells and a rope around the high priest's ankle so they could hear if he was still moving and pull him out if he died.

Years later, a permanent Tabernacle, called the temple, was built in the capital city of Jerusalem as a symbol of God's presence remaining with the people. Throughout Israel's history, the presence of God would enter the Holy of Holies in the temple, shielded from humans behind a thick curtain.

READER 4:

It was now about noon, and darkness came over the whole land until three in the afternoon, for the sun stopped shining. And the curtain of the temple was torn in two. Jesus called out with a loud voice, "Father, into your hands I commit my spirit." When he had said this, he breathed his last. —Luke 23:44-46

When Jesus died on the cross, the temple veil was torn in half—from the top to the bottom. Only God could have carried out such an incredible feat because the veil was too tall and thick for humans to tear it.

As the veil was torn, the Holy of Holies was exposed. The priests working in the temple that day must have been shocked and terrified. Can you imagine?

*HANDOUTS

THE TABERNACLE Station 8: The Holy of Holies and the Veil

READER 1:

This amazing act is good news for all people. The torn veil symbolizes Jesus' body being broken for us, opening a new way for us to come to God. As Jesus cried out on the cross, "It is finished" (John 19:30), he was indeed proclaiming that the age of animal sacrifices was over. The ultimate and final sacrifice had been made.

Look at the veil. How do you think it would have felt to be a priest, unable to see the other side?

Take a moment and thank your High Priest, Jesus, who made it possible for you to enter the Holy of Holies along with him and to be with God.

But now Jesus, our High Priest, has been given a ministry that is far superior to the old priesthood, for he is the one who mediates for us a far better covenant with God, based on better promises. —Hebrews 8:6 (NLT)

Remove your shoes as a sign of reverence to God.

Then walk around the veil and sit down on the floor next to the candle.

Spend a few minutes in prayer, thanking God for Jesus and letting God know how thankful you are to be on the other side of the veil.

After a few minutes, put your handouts in a neat stack for the next group and continue on to Station 9.

THE TABERNACLE
Station 9
The Ark of the Covenant and the Mercy Seat

READER 1:

Within the Holy of Holies was a special wooden chest called the ark of the covenant. The ark was made of wood and overlaid with pure gold—inside and out.

On top of the ark, there was a gold cover called the mercy seat where the presence of God rested. This cover was elaborately decorated with two gold cherubim (angels) on each end, facing each other with outstretched wings that covered the top of the ark. The entire cover was created from one piece of pure gold.

The mercy seat was God's actual dwelling place in the Tabernacle—the throne where God appeared in an unapproachable light. God's presence among the people of Israel was what made them a unique nation, different from all the others.

> **The priests could not enter the temple of the LORD because the glory of the LORD filled it. When all the Israelites saw the fire coming down and the glory of the LORD above the temple, they knelt on the pavement with their faces to the ground, and they worshiped and gave thanks to the LORD, saying, "He is good; his love endures forever." —2 Chronicles 7:2-3**

READER 2:

Protected inside the ark of the covenant weren't treasures or precious gems, but three unusual items: A jar filled with manna, a staff, and stone tablets. To represent these items, we've provided a table with bread, a stick, and two stones.

BREAD

> **So Moses said to Aaron, "Take a jar and put an omer of manna in it. Then place it before the LORD to be kept for the generations to come." As the LORD commanded Moses, Aaron put the manna with the tablets of the covenant law, so that it might be preserved. —Exodus 16:33-34**

God provided manna, a honey-flavored bread-like food, for the Israelites when they grumbled during their wanderings in the desert. It was sweet bread from heaven! God faithfully provided this food daily, but the people were ungrateful. They complained and wanted something more. The jar of manna in the ark was a painful reminder that the Israelites had been ungrateful for God's provision.

A STICK

READER 3:

The LORD said to Moses, "Put back Aaron's staff in front of the ark of the covenant law, to be kept as a sign to the rebellious. This will put an end to their grumbling against me, so that they will not die." —Numbers 17:10

Out of jealousy, the Israelites rebelled against their high priest Aaron (Moses' brother). To affirm God's choice of Aaron as their priest, God made Aaron's staff bud with flower blossoms and almonds! This staff was placed inside the ark as a reminder that the Israelites had rebelled against God's established authority.

TWO STONES

READER 4:

The tablets were the work of God; the writing was the writing of God, engraved on the tablets. —Exodus 32:16

[God said to the people of Israel,] "Now if you obey me fully and keep my covenant, then out of all nations you will be my treasured possession. Although the whole earth is mine, you will be for me a kingdom of priests and a holy nation." —Exodus 19:5-6

God chose the Israelites as a special people who were called to live differently in the world. God also provided specific instructions, called laws and commands, to help the people know how to live God's way. God wrote the commands on two stone tablets with a finger. But the Israelites

THE TABERNACLE Station 9: The Ark of the Covenant and the Mercy Seat

still struggled and turned away from God, choosing their own selfish and destructive ways. There-fore, the stone tablets inside the ark were another reminder that the Israelites had failed at God's way of living.

READER 5:

The three objects in the ark of the covenant represented Israel's struggle to follow God. As God filled the Holy of Holies and sat on the mercy seat above the ark, these failures were covered over. God himself provided a way for them to be covered!

Look at the bread…take a moment and quietly confess to God the times when you've been ungrateful for his provision. *(Pause.)*

Now take a minute to look at the stick…quietly confess to God the times you've rebelled against the people God has placed in authority over you (parents, teachers, church leaders, and so on). *(Pause.)*

Next, look at the stones…take a moment and quietly confess to God the times you've chosen to go against God's way of living. *(Pause.)*

Gather in a circle around the table containing the three items. Have everyone in the group hold a part of the white sheet high above the table for a moment.

Pray together, thanking God for his divine action to cover over your disobedience and unfaith-fulness. Drop the sheet over the table to cover these items in the same way that Jesus covers over our failures.

After a few moments, carefully remove the sheet and fold it up for the next group. Then put your handouts in a neat stack and continue on to the next station. On the way, adults should pick up one balloon and markers for each person in their group.

10 THE TABERNACLE
Station 10
The Release and Group Interaction

Take a red balloon and have the group members carefully write their names on it. Don't pop it! And make sure someone hangs on to the balloon at all times as you head outside.

READER 1:
In the same way that the scapegoat (azazel) carried away the rebellion of Israel, Jesus carried away our wrongdoing.

Everyone place your hands on this balloon. *(This may require you to huddle tightly together.)*

Now one person should pray aloud, expressing gratitude to God for the freedom we have from selfishness and shame. Together, release the balloon and watch it float up into the sky. Keep watching it until it disappears. Then everyone should find a quiet place to journal about the experience. After a few minutes, bring the group back together to discuss the following questions.

JOURNAL, THEN DISCUSS

- What were you thinking or feeling while you watched the balloon float out of sight?
- What part of the Tabernacle impacted you the most? Why?
- What did you learn for the first time today? What do you wonder about?
- What does the Tabernacle show us about God?
- What did the Tabernacle show you about yourself?

Put your handouts in a neat stack for the next group.

THE KINGDOM

DEVELOPED BY MICHAEL NOVELLI

*INSTRUCTIONS

DESCRIPTION

The Kingdom Experience is designed to offer a better sense of what God's kingdom is and explore how we can join in God's kingdom activity. Stations will move participants from creative response to reflection and discussion about what it means for us to be a part of God's kingdom.

LOCATIONS AND LOGISTICS

- I've set up this experience both outdoors and indoors. I used handmade signs displayed on easels to delineate the stations. If you choose to do this, please add to your materials list an easel and a sign for each station.

- A couple of the stations require you to find and print photos ahead of time (recommended images to purchase from iStock Photo are available on accompanying CD). An inexpensive and quick way to do this is to take them to Walgreens (or a similar drug store that offers photo development services) and print them out. You can even upload them, pay for them online, and then pick them up a few hours later. This can save you a lot of time, printer ink, and hassle.

GROUP SIZE

This can be done with a whole group of up to 40 people. That being said, I believe this will work best with smaller groups of 20 or fewer people. Otherwise it may be hard to hear one another during the discussion.

STATIONS (STOPPING POINTS)

STATION 1: THE MYSTERIES OF THE KINGDOM

LOCATION AND PREPARATION

Participants will get into groups of two to complete the Situation Puzzle handout. Provide enough space for them to spread out for this activity, and then regroup to discuss and read the handout all together. This station could work well indoors or outdoors.

MATERIALS

- Copies of the Station 1 handouts for every participant (available on accompanying CD).
- Copies of the Situation Puzzle handouts for each pair of participants (available on accompanying CD).
- Pens.

STATION 2: RHYTHMS OF GOD'S KINGDOM

LOCATION AND PREPARATION

Participants will receive a small stone to use as a tactile device while in prayer. Then they'll spread out and engage in a *lectio divina* activity using the Beatitudes.

MATERIALS

- Small, smooth stones in a bowl or spread out on a table.
- Copies of the Station 2 handouts for every participant (available on accompanying CD).
- Pens.

STATION 3: KINGDOMS IN OUR CULTURE

LOCATION AND PREPARATION

Participants will use Post-its and magazine clippings to identify characteristics of kingdoms from our culture. You'll need a large bulletin board or poster for the groups to attach their observations. They'll think in terms of the following categories: Wealth and success, fashion and consumerism, popularity and vanity, and power and force (images to represent each of these areas are recommended for purchase on accompanying CD in this station's instructions). This station may work best indoors.

MATERIALS

- A long bulletin board or four large posters on sturdy easels.

- Small, smooth stones in a bowl or spread out on a table.

- Copies of the Station 3 handouts for every participant (available on accompanying CD).

- Four images representing wealth and success, fashion and consumerism, popularity and vanity, and power and force that you can use as signs to identify areas for your brainstorming time (recommended images to purchase from iStock Photo are available on accompanying CD in this station's instructions).

- Dark-colored Post-its—enough for each person to have several.

- Light-colored Post-its—enough for each person to have several.

- Pens.

- Magazines that cover current cultural trends and represent wealth and success, fashion and consumerism, popularity and vanity, and power and force, such as *People, Us, Newsweek, Seventeen, Rolling Stone, Guns & Ammo, Popular Mechanics, Teen Vogue,* and *CosmoGirl.*

- Several pairs of scissors.

- Rolls of clear tape or pushpins to post the magazine images.

STATION 4: KINGDOM PARABLES

LOCATION AND PREPARATION

Participants will get into groups of two to examine a parable and share their observations with the group. Kingdom Parable Cards containing questions are available on accompanying CD. (Recommended images to purchase form iStock Photo are on accompanying CD in this station's instructions.) This station could work well indoors or outdoors.

OPTIONAL IDEA

To add a creative flair to this idea, you can string up a clothesline in your meeting room and hang the pictures from it with clothespins. Include the pictures from Station 6 to create a continuous visual of kingdom pictures for the entire experience.

MATERIALS

- Parable Pictures—two for every pair of participants (recommended images to purchase from iStock Photo are available on accompanying CD in this station's instructions). (Background cards are available on CD.) Participants can use the same parable, so duplicate as needed.

- Kingdom Parable Cards—with questions and a spot for each of the Parable Pictures.

- Copies of the Station 4 handouts for every participant (available on accompanying CD).

- Pens.

- Optional: A long, thin rope and clothespins for each picture.

- Bibles—one for every pair of participants.

STATION 5: THE GROWING KINGDOM

LOCATION AND PREPARATION

- Participants will explore how the kingdom grows from something small to something large. They'll make pretzels in groups of six to eight, following the simple instructions available on accompanying CD. If you don't have the time or means to make pretzels,

I've provided a simpler alternative idea using flowerpots and seeds. (See the next station's instructions.)

- Allow some extra time for this experience, as the dough will need to rise for an hour. And then it will take time for the participants to shape and bake the pretzels. Only the first step of the pretzel-making process is done during Station 5. You'll come back to the final steps after you've completed the rest of the stations. Have a party at the end of the Kingdom Experience so everyone can enjoy the pretzels. This station works best indoors, since it requires an oven.

MATERIALS

- Pretzel-Making Instructions handout—several for each group of six to eight (available on accompanying CD).

- Materials and ingredients for making pretzels—included on the Pretzel-Making Instructions handout (available on accompanying CD).

- An oven.

- Copies of the Station 5 handouts for every participant (available on accompanying CD).

- Pens.

STATION 5:
THE GROWING KINGDOM—ALTERNATIVE IDEA
LOCATION AND PREPARATION

Participants will explore how the kingdom grows from something small to something large. Each person will plant a seed in a pot while discussing the parable of the mustard seed.

MATERIALS

- Small flowerpots filled with soil—one for each group (or two for large groups).

- One small bowl of seeds—preferably for something that will grow quickly.

- Copies of the Station 5 handouts for every participant (available on accompanying CD).

- Pens.

STATION 6: THE KINGDOM OF THE FORGOTTEN
LOCATION AND PREPARATION

Participants will examine the stories of people who are considered the "least of these" and share their observations. Kingdom of the Forgotten Cards containing questions are available on accompanying CD. (Recommended images to purchase from iStock Photo are on accompanying CD in this station's instructions.) This station could work well indoors or outdoors.

OPTIONAL IDEA

To add a creative flair to this idea, you can string up a clothesline in your meeting room and hang the pictures from it with clothespins. Include the pictures from Station 4 to create a continuous visual of kingdom pictures for the entire experience.

MATERIALS

- Pictures of the forgotten—one for each participant (recommended images to purchase from iStock Photo are available on accompanying CD in this station's instructions). Participants can have the same picture, if needed.

- Kingdom of the Forgotten cards—with stories, questions, and a spot for each of the Forgotten Pictures.

- Copies of the Station 6 handouts for every participant (available on accompanying CD).

- Pens.

- Optional: A long, thin rope and clothespins for each picture.

STATION 7: THE KINGDOM MISSION
LOCATION AND PREPARATION

Participants will reflect on all of the kingdom snapshots they've seen during this experience. Allow time for them to silently walk around and look at the pictures and objects from the other stations once more. This station could work well indoors or outdoors.

MATERIALS

- Copies of the Station 7 handouts for every participant (available on accompanying CD).

- Pens.

THE KINGDOM
Introduction

EVERYONE READ SILENTLY

This is an important time to…

- Connect with God and
- Connect with others in meaningful ways.

This time requires you to…

- Slow down and turn off your cell phone.
- Enter into a different pace of life.
- Speak quietly and act respectfully.
- Think deeply and engage your mind and heart.
- Be open to what God has for you.

We hope that through this experience you'll see how your story is connected to and a continuation of a bigger Story that began thousands of years ago.

Pray quietly and ask God to help you enter the story.

You will enter this experience with your entire group. At each station, different people from your group will read parts aloud. You don't have to read if you don't want to, but as many people as possible should read and help guide the experience.

*HANDOUTS

For this first part, your group should stand in a circle, read, listen, and discuss.

READER 1:

Jesus was always talking about God's kingdom. In fact, his entire life was focused on pointing people to God and God's kingdom, which is mentioned more than 50 times in the Gospel of Matthew alone.

DISCUSS

- What do you think of when you hear the word *kingdom*?

EVERYONE READ OUT LOUD

From then on Jesus began to preach, "Repent of your sins and turn to God, for the Kingdom of Heaven is near." —Matthew 4:17 (NLT)

READER 2:

A kingdom is a community of people who live under a certain order and are led by a king. In Jesus' day, "kingdom" language was pretty common because there were actually kings and kingdoms. So the people understood this system of ruling. Kingdom dwellers also understood that it was a shared community, meaning that all of their possessions, money, time, and land—even their very lives—belonged to the kingdom.

READER 3:

When Jewish people heard Jesus' kingdom message, many believed he was trying to build a militia to overpower the corrupt government that was ruled by Roman and Jewish leaders. Some hoped Jesus was their long-awaited Messiah coming to reestablish Israel as a strong nation and military power.

READER 4:

THE KINGDOM Introduction

About that time the disciples came to Jesus and asked, "Who is greatest in the Kingdom of Heaven?" Jesus called a little child to him and put the child among them. Then he said, "I tell you the truth, unless you turn from your sins and become like little children, you will never get into the Kingdom of Heaven. So anyone who becomes as humble as this little child is the greatest in the Kingdom of Heaven." —Matthew 18:1-4 (NLT)

"But among you it will be different. Whoever wants to be a leader among you must be your servant, and whoever wants to be first among you must become your slave. For even the Son of Man came not to be served but to serve others and to give his life as a ransom for many." —Matthew 20:26-28 (NLT)

READER 5:

Once, having been asked by the Pharisees when the kingdom of God would come, Jesus replied, "The kingdom of God does not come with your careful observation, nor will people say, 'Here it is,' or 'There it is,' because the kingdom of God is within you." —Luke 17:20-21

DISCUSS

- What kind of kingdom were the Jewish people hoping for?
- What words or images would you use to describe God's kingdom?
- Where did Jesus say the kingdom of God is? What do you think it takes to be a part of it?
- How should our lives be different if "the kingdom of God is within you"?

After your discussion, please continue to the next station. (You may keep this handout.)

*HANDOUTS

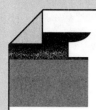

THE KINGDOM
Station 1
The Mysteries of the Kingdom

Get in groups of two or three and pick up a Situation Puzzle handout. See which group can get the most correct answers in three minutes. If you don't know an answer, go on to the next puzzle.

DISCUSS

- What does it take to solve these kinds of puzzles?

- How do you think God's kingdom might be like this?

READER 1:

To discover God's kingdom may require us to look at it from a different perspective. Many of us may immediately think that "God's kingdom" is just referring to heaven. However, the Israelites were looking for a military kingdom that would overthrow the Roman Empire. Both of these viewpoints miss what God's kingdom is really about and require us to search deeper.

> [Jesus] told them, "...to those who can't see [God's kingdom] yet, everything comes in stories, creating readiness, nudging them toward receptive insight." —Mark 4:10-12 (The Message)

READER 2:

God's kingdom isn't something we can easily explain or grasp. In order to see the kingdom, we must search for it—chase after it, enjoy it, marvel at it, live in it, and let it shape us. It's often in the midst of our wonders, doubts, and questions that we begin to discover the depth of who God is.

READER 3:

God's kingdom is like a riddle—it turns our thinking upside down: The peasants are given power, the first become last, foolishness becomes profound, the poor are actually rich, children are mature, and the weak become strong.

READER 4:

This was Jesus' message—God's kingdom is a mystery for us to ponder, searching the intentions of our heart in order to understand. It's a hidden treasure, and we need the help of the Divine to unlock it.

Are you ready to explore the kingdom of God?

Our hope is that we'll find life in the kingdom and the kingdom will live in us.

READER 5:

"No eye has seen, no ear has heard, and no mind has imagined what God has prepared for those who love him." But it was to us that God revealed these things by his Spirit. For his Spirit searches out everything and shows us God's deep secrets. —1 Corinthians 2:9-10 (NLT)

READER 6:

Now take a moment and pray. Cover your eyes with your hands as you do so, asking God to reveal to you through the Holy Spirit the mysteries of God's kingdom.

After your prayer, please continue to the next station. (You may keep this handout.)

THE KINGDOM
Station 2
Rhythms of God's Kingdom

READER 1:

Jesus' best-known teaching is called the Beatitudes, which means "happiness and completeness found in God." This was Jesus' masterpiece, a powerful message that defines the values of God's kingdom.

As we enter this next prayer exercise, pick up a smooth stone and hold it in your hand as a reminder of the wholeness that God offers in the kingdom.

READER 2:

Lectio divina is Latin for "divine reading." This ancient practice helps us to slow down, listen, and pray, looking for God to reveal himself to us through God's Word. During this exercise make sure you find a place where you can concentrate and won't be distracted by others.

READER 3:

We'll follow these steps to guide our time:

1. READ *(Lectio)*: Slowly read the passage several times.

2. REFLECT *(Meditatio)*: What word or phrase stands out to you? What speaks to you directly? Write your thoughts next to the verses.

3. PRAY *(Oratio)*: Open your palms as you pray. Let God know that your heart, mind, and soul are open to hearing from God now.

4. LISTEN *(Contemplatio)*: Listen for God to speak to or guide you in some way. Don't rush this listening time. If your mind wanders, refocus by asking God to help you sense God's nearness.

Repeat this four-step process three times or go back to a part of it that was meaningful to you and repeat it to help you connect with God. The goal of this time is to release all of your expectations and become more aware of God's presence.

THE KINGDOM Station 2: Rhythms of God's Kingdom

EVERYONE READ SILENTLY

Before you begin reading, take a moment to clear your mind right now. Take some deep breaths and pray, inviting the Holy Spirit to speak to you and help you focus during your prayer time.

You will begin this exercise now and then gather together in about 15 minutes. Let's begin with step one, *Lectio*. For the first reading, an adult will read the Beatitudes out loud. The other readings will be done silently on your own.

The Beatitudes

One day as he saw the crowds gathering, Jesus went up on the mountainside and sat down. His disciples gathered around him, and he began to teach them.

"God blesses those who are poor and realize their need for him,

for the Kingdom of Heaven is theirs.

God blesses those who mourn,

for they will be comforted.

God blesses those who are humble,

for they will inherit the whole earth.

God blesses those who hunger and thirst for justice,

for they will be satisfied.

God blesses those who are merciful,

for they will be shown mercy.

God blesses those whose hearts are pure,

for they will see God.

God blesses those who work for peace,

for they will be called the children of God.

God blesses those who are persecuted for doing right,

for the Kingdom of Heaven is theirs." —Matthew 5:1-10 (NLT)

*HANDOUTS

JOURNAL & DISCUSS

- What words or phrases stood out to you the most?

- What did you notice for the first time?

- What did you learn about what God is like?

- What do you think it means to live in rhythm with God?

- How do the Beatitudes motivate you to live differently?

Gather back together as a group after 10 to 15 minutes. Discuss your responses that you journaled here. After your sharing time, please continue to the next station. (You may keep this handout.)

THE KINGDOM
Station 3
Kingdoms in Our Culture

READER 1:

As we've already explored, a kingdom is a certain *order* that people follow—a way of life. And any kingdom—way of life—has its own set of values and priorities.

READER 2:

Take a moment to look at the four images. They represent some of the "kingdoms" in our culture and world: Wealth and success, fashion and consumerism, popularity and vanity, and power and force.

These areas may have a rightful place and value, but the problem is that we're often drawn to center our lives around them.

BRAINSTORM

- What images, people, or words immediately pop into your mind when you think about the "kingdoms" in these pictures?

- What are the values and priorities of this way of life?

On dark-colored Post-its, every group member should write a response to each of the four "kingdoms" represented on the four posters and then attach them next to the appropriate images. Another option is to cut out applicable pictures from magazines and tape them to the posters.

DISCUSS

- Who (people) or what (values) seems to "rule" in these areas in our culture?

- How do you see people being consumed by these things in your school or neighborhood?

- How do people make these "kingdoms" the center or goal of their lives?

- Why is that not a good goal to have? Where does that lead us?

*HANDOUTS

- How are these "kingdoms" tempting us to live?
- Which one of these four "kingdoms" is the most tempting for you personally?
- How can God restore some of these words and images for good?

BRAINSTORM

- Can you see how these kingdoms stand in contrast to God's kingdom as it's described in the Beatitudes?

READER 3:

For each of the four "kingdoms" portrayed on the posters, take 30 seconds and write your answer to the following question on light-colored Post-its: *How is God's kingdom different than (have the opposite values of) the "kingdoms" in each picture?* Then place the Post-its on the appropriate poster. You could either write words or draw pictures that describe your answers. For example, you could write SEEKING GOD'S KINGDOM = GENEROSITY and stick the Post-it onto the "wealth and success" poster.

EVERYONE PRAY OUT LOUD

God,

We're distracted by so much that this world has to offer.

Help us see that your kingdom is the only one that brings life and wholeness.

Give us strength to live in your ways and be a light for you.

Amen.

Please continue on to the next station. (You may keep this handout.)

THE KINGDOM
Station 4
Kingdom Parables

READER 1:

Jesus taught about the kingdom of God using short stories with profound meanings, called parables. In Latin the word *parable* means "parallel story."

> Jesus always used stories and illustrations like these when speaking to the crowds. In fact, he never spoke to them without using such parables. This fulfilled what God had spoken through the prophet: "I will speak to you in parables. I will explain things hidden since the creation of the world." —Matthew 13:34-35 (NLT)

Using everyday characters and objects as powerful word pictures, Jesus reached the hearts of his listeners through their imaginations. The meanings of Jesus' parables were sometimes obvious—and other times they were hidden.

READER 2:

> [Jesus'] disciples came and asked him, "Why do you use parables when you talk to the people?"

> He replied, "You are permitted to understand the secrets of the Kingdom of Heaven, but others are not. To those who listen to my teaching, more understanding will be given, and they will have an abundance of knowledge...But blessed are your eyes, because they see; and your ears, because they hear." —Matthew 13:10-12, 16 (NLT)

DISCUSS

- Why do you think Jesus used parables to communicate God's message?

- What does it take to understand Jesus' parables?

*HANDOUTS

READER 3:

Get in groups of two and select two different Parable Pictures.

Read the verses carefully and discuss the questions provided. Be ready to share your insights about your parables with the entire group.

After several minutes, ask for volunteers to hold up their cards and share their observations. When the sharing time is complete, move on to the next station. (You may keep this handout.)

THE TABERNACLE
Station 5
The Growing Kingdom

READER 1:

> Again [Jesus] asked, "What shall I compare the kingdom of God to? It is like yeast that a woman took and mixed into about sixty pounds of flour until it worked all through the dough." —Luke 13:20-21

Jesus compared the growing kingdom of God, which we're a part of, to yeast. The kingdom emerges in and through us as a community whenever we submit ourselves to God's ways. But we cannot do this on our own; we need each other's support and the guidance of the Holy Spirit.

READER 2:

Now we'll prepare some dough to make pretzels, and we'll be spreading yeast into it. Why do we add yeast to the dough?

Complete Making Pretzels—Step One: Prepare the dough now from the pretzel making instructions. Allow about an hour for the dough to rise, then bake them. Have a party after your kingdom experience and eat your pretzels together.

READER 3:

Yeast makes bread lighter, softer, tastier, and twice as large as the dough it started out as. The interesting thing is that yeast is alive. Yeast is a growing culture, and when it's given the right temperature and moisture, it multiplies like crazy.

Complete "Making Pretzels—Step One" by preparing the pretzel dough. Allow about an hour for the dough to rise, then shape and bake them.

DISCUSS

- How is God's kingdom like yeast? How is it alive?
- How can something small make a big difference in God's kingdom?

*HANDOUTS

- How do you think God's kingdom grows or spreads?
- How does the kingdom grow and spread in your own life?

READER 4:

Later on we'll shape, bake, add toppings to, and then eat our pretzels. Yum!

Say a brief prayer together, asking God to reveal his kingdom through your group. After your prayer, please continue to the next station. (You may keep this handout.)

THE KINGDOM
Station 5
The Growing Kingdom (Alternative Idea)

READER 1:

> Then Jesus asked, "What is the kingdom of God like? What shall I compare it to? It is like a mustard seed, which a man took and planted in his garden. It grew and became a tree, and the birds perched in its branches." —Luke 13:18-19

These seeds represent the growing kingdom of God of which we're a part. The kingdom emerges in and through us as a community whenever we submit ourselves to God's ways. But we cannot do this on our own; we need each other's support and the guidance of the Holy Spirit.

READER 2:

Now we'll each take a seed and plant it in the soil of our pot. As we do this, let's talk about the parable of the mustard seed.

- Why do you think Jesus taught in parables?
- How might God's kingdom be like a small seed?
- How do you think the kingdom grows or spreads?
- How do you think God's kingdom is (or will be) like a large tree with long branches?
- What else did you notice about this parable?

At the end of your discussion, say a brief prayer together, asking God to reveal his kingdom through your group. Take your plant with you as a reminder that God's kingdom is in you—and you are in it. Proceed to the next station. (You may keep this handout.)

6 THE KINGDOM
Station 6
The Kingdom of the Forgotten

READER 1:

When reading the Beatitudes, we discover a hard-to-explain mystery found in Jesus' life and message: Those whom society considers worthless and unlovable, God sees as being the greatest and the closest to God and God's kingdom.

EVERYONE READ OUT LOUD

Hasn't God chosen the poor in this world to be rich in faith? Aren't they the ones who will inherit the Kingdom he promised to those who love him? —James 2:5 (NLT)

And the King will say, "I tell you the truth, when you did it to one of the least of these my brothers and sisters, you were doing it to me!" —Matthew 25:40

READER 2:

Whenever we encounter those whom society considers to be "the least"—the poor, sick, elderly, and helpless—we're to look at them as we'd look at Jesus: As someone who has much to reveal to us about God. That's part of the beautiful mystery of the kingdom—the least are the ones who reveal God the most.

READER 3:

"I believe that the great tragedy of the church is not that rich Christians do not care about the poor, but that they do not know the poor. Yet if we are called to live the new community for which Christ was crucified, we cannot remain strangers to one another. Jesus demands that we live in a very different way."[21] —Shane Claiborne, author of *An Irresistible Revolution*

21 Shane Claiborne, "Downward Mobility in an Upscale World," *The Other Side* (November 1, 2000), http://speakingoffaith.publicradio.org/programs/newmonastics/claiborne_downwardmobility.shtml

THE KINGDOM Station 6: The Kingdom of the Forgotten

READER 4:

In front of you are pictures of people who represent "the least of these," of whom Jesus spoke. While their stories may be fictional, they symbolize people near and far to whom we can bring God's kingdom and—maybe more importantly—within whom we can *find* God's kingdom.

Pick up one of the pictures. Slow your mind. Spend two to three minutes looking at the picture and thinking about the questions on it. Ask God to reveal to you how you might learn from the person in the picture.

DISCUSS

Hold up your picture so the rest of the group can see it and summarize the story.

- How did the story make you feel?

- How do you think you'd respond to that person?

- What questions would you ask that person?

- Why do you think God has a special affinity for the poor, downcast, hungry, merciful, peacemakers, and persecuted?

- What does it mean to have a kingdom perspective—to see people through Jesus' eyes?

- Christians often give to and serve the poor and forgotten while keeping them at a distance. What would it take for you to really get to know a poor or forgotten person in your neighborhood or city?

- What can we learn from a poor person? How might they reveal God's kingdom to us?

- How might our group begin to build relationships with the poor, sick, elderly, forgotten, and helpless in our community?

As a group, pray that God would bring about opportunities for you to reach out to the forgotten in your community and grow in each of you a deeper sense of compassion. (You may keep this handout.)

*HANDOUTS

7 THE KINGDOM
Station 7
The Kingdom Mission

READER 1:

> [Jesus read,] "The Spirit of the Lord is upon me, for he has anointed me to bring Good News to the poor. He has sent me to proclaim that captives will be released, that the blind will see, that the oppressed will be set free, and that the time of the Lord's favor has come." —Luke 4:18-19 (NLT)

This was Jesus' mission on earth—to join God in restoring us to wholeness. The life and ministry that Jesus embodied on earth is now given to us.

READER 2:

> Therefore, if anyone is in Christ, the new creation has come: The old has gone, the new is here! All this is from God, who reconciled us to himself through Christ and gave us the ministry of reconciliation: that God was reconciling the world to himself in Christ, not counting people's sins against them. And he has committed to us the message of reconciliation. —2 Corinthians 5:17-19

Jesus empowers his followers—the church—to continue to reveal the kingdom to others. God has sent us to continue in the way of Jesus and give the world a glimpse of what living in God's ways—in God's kingdom—looks like.

READER 3:

We're to bring restoration to all of God's creation. That means we have a responsibility to care for the earth and everything that lives here. We can bring new life to that which has been forgotten, wounded, polluted, or neglected—to meet the needs of a hurting and fallen world.

THE KINGDOM Station 7: The Kingdom Mission

DISCUSS

- How would our world look if God's kingdom came in its full potential?
- What would be different?

EVERYONE READ OUT LOUD

Imagine a world where...

We share with those in need, and no one goes hungry or cold.

All living things are treated with great value.

Joy replaces tears and depression; indifference turns to compassion.

Peace and dignity replace our struggle for power. Wars and conflicts cease.

All are free from the influence of insecurity, anxiety, and fear.

Forgiveness is extended and relationships are restored to wholeness.

Everyone has a place to live and a community to support and care for them.

People are reconnected with their Creator, reflecting God's nature in all they do.

Imagine a world where all surrender to Jesus as King and follow in his ways of love.

Together, we can help make that world a reality.

JOURNAL

Take time to quietly walk around and look at all of the parable and kingdom pictures once more. Soak in all of the faces and stories. Then go off by yourself and use the following questions to journal your thoughts and ideas about this experience.

- What did you notice? What stands out to you?
- After all of the different ways we've looked at the kingdom of God, what do you think it's all about?

*HANDOUTS

- What would it take for you to live in the kingdom?

- What would it take for our group to live in the kingdom?

Gather back together as a group after 10 to 15 minutes. Discuss your journal responses. Then conclude the experience with a group reading of The Lord's Prayer.

EVERYONE PRAY OUT LOUD

Our Father who is in heaven,

Hallowed be Your name.

Your kingdom come

Your will be done,

On earth as it is in heaven.

Give us this day our daily bread.

And forgive us our debts, as we also have forgiven our debtors.

And do not lead us into temptation, but deliver us from evil.

[For Yours is the kingdom and the power and the glory forever. Amen.]

—Matthew 6:9-13 (NASB)

(You may keep this handout.)

JOURNEY TO THE CROSS

DEVELOPED BY FAITH BOSLAND
ADAPTED BY MICHAEL NOVELLI

*INSTRUCTIONS

DESCRIPTION

Meditating on the events of Jesus' final days and his resurrection can be profound. The challenge for most of us is shutting out the noise and distractions of everyday life long enough to quiet our souls and listen to the Spirit of God. You can set up an inspiring way to interactively meditate on Jesus' journey to the cross by creating stations for contemplation around your facility. This design has 13 stations, most of which can accommodate approximately five people at a time.

This experience is unique from the rest of the ones described in the book in that it will be done in silence.

LOCATIONS AND LOGISTICS

Allow several days to gather props and plan the layout. You will need several hours to set up the stations.

Have someone standing by to usher people in—one at a time. The first station is the only one that's best experienced individually. Since everyone begins at the first station, you need a plan for staggering the start. Expect people to spend anywhere from an hour to 90 minutes walking through the Journey to the Cross Experience.

- Clearly mark the way to each station with masking-tape arrows on the floor or signs on the wall so no one is confused or wandering around.

- Space the stations fairly far apart to minimize distractions and allow room for several people at each station.

- Have someone occasionally relight the candles at Station 10, Jesus' Death, so participants will always find a lit candle to extinguish.

- Offer a place where people can continue to listen to the music or interact quietly after they finish the Journey to the Cross. They may want to sit in a pew by themselves or return to the worship area where they began. People often want to hang out for a while after finishing the Journey.

- If you have a large event, plan multiple locations of the Journey to the Cross so more people can experience it and not be rushed.

- Participants will keep the handouts from each station, as they'll be asked to write on them at several of the stations.

GROUP SIZE

This design has 13 stations, most of which can accommodate approximately five people at a time. Participants can go at their own pace and will work through the stations and handouts completely on their own.

STATIONS (STOPPING POINTS)

STATION 1: OUTER NOISE

MATERIALS

- A TV tuned to static.

- Station 1 handouts for participants to keep (available on accompanying CD).

- Pens.

STATION 2: GOD IN THE FLESH
MATERIALS

- A pair of men's sandals.
- Station 2 handouts for participants to keep (available on accompanying CD).
- Pens.

STATION 3: MARY ANOINTS JESUS
MATERIALS

- Cotton balls.
- A medicine dropper.
- Scented oil (can be found in the potpourri or air freshener aisles at Target).
- Station 3 handouts for participants to keep (available on accompanying CD).
- Pens.

STATION 4: JUDAS AGREES TO BETRAY JESUS
MATERIALS

- Coins—exotic or ancient ones, if you can get them.
- Station 4 handouts for participants to keep (available on accompanying CD).
- Pens.

STATION 5: THE LAST SUPPER
MATERIALS

- Pita bread.
- Olive oil in a bowl.
- Station 5 handouts for participants to keep (available on accompanying CD).
- Pens.

STATION 6: GETHSEMANE

MATERIALS

- A pitcher of grape juice.
- Cups.
- Several large, leafy plants to give a garden ambiance.
- Station 6 handouts for participants to keep (available on accompanying CD).
- Pens.

STATION 7: JESUS' ARREST

MATERIALS

- Prayer journals.
- Markers.
- Rope.
- Station 7 handouts for participants to keep (available on accompanying CD).
- Pens.

STATION 8: JESUS' TRIAL

LOCATION AND PREPARATION

If possible, locate Station 8 in a balcony or other high point. Place the robe and crown in a lower area where participants can gaze down on them.

MATERIALS

- Prayer journals.
- Markers.
- Purple cloth.
- A crown of thorns.
- Station 8 handouts for participants to keep (available on accompanying CD).
- Pens.

STATION 9: JESUS' CRUCIFIXION

LOCATION AND PREPARATION

Set up Station 9 in the main area. It's effective to plan the path from Station 8 to Station 9 so people focus on the cross as they're walking toward it, even if it's not the most direct way between the two stations. For example, arrange Station 9 at the front altar of the sanctuary. Beginning at Station 8, tape directional arrows to the floor to lead participants to the back of the room, down the main aisle, and toward the front of the room. At Station 9, participants will hammer nails into the cross, so be sure you choose a cross that's appropriate for that purpose.

MATERIALS

- A wooden cross.
- Nails.
- Hammers.
- Paper and pens.
- Station 9 handouts for participants to keep (available on accompanying CD).

STATION 10: JESUS' DEATH

LOCATION AND PREPARATION

Have someone occasionally relight the candles at Station 10 so participants will always find a lit candle to extinguish.

MATERIALS

- Candles.
- A candlesnuffer.
- Matches.
- Station 10 handouts for participants to keep (available on accompanying CD).
- Pens.

STATION 11: JESUS' BURIAL

MATERIALS

- A large rock (about the size of a grapefruit would be good).
- Station 11 handouts for participants to keep (available on accompanying CD).
- Pens.

STATION 12: JESUS' RESURRECTION

MATERIALS

- White cloth draped to look like grave clothes.
- Station 12 handouts for participants to keep (available on accompanying CD).
- Pens.

STATION 13: CROSSROADS

LOCATION AND PREPARATION

Set up Station 13 so when people look in the mirror, they see themselves, the cross behind them, and some of the stations of the Journey.

MATERIALS

- Markers.
- A mirror.
- Station 13 handouts for participants to keep (available on accompanying CD).
- Pens.

JOURNEY TO THE CROSS
Introduction

EVERYONE READ SILENTLY

This is an important time to connect with God. This time requires you to…

- Slow down and turn off your cell phone.

- Enter into a different pace of life.

- Speak quietly and act respectfully.

- Think deeply and engage your mind and heart.

- Be open to what God has for you.

We hope that through this experience you'll see how your story is connected to and a continuation of a bigger Story that began thousands of years ago.

You will enter this experience on your own. Today is a time to slow down, to leave the busyness of your life at the entrance, and to focus on Jesus. Take your time. Read slowly. Let the words of reflection sink in.

Spend as long as you want at each station. If you're drawn to stay at a particular spot for a long time, you're free to do so. Move on to the next station whenever you're ready. Don't feel pressured to move if others leave a station before you do.

If more than three people are already at the next station, pause where you are until someone leaves. You may respond to God by writing your thoughts on the handouts provided at each station. You can write a word, write a prayer, draw a picture—whatever you want to do. You may feel like writing on some pages and not on others. That's okay.

This Journey to the Cross is not about agendas or meeting anyone's expectations. It's simply a time and a place for you to draw close to Jesus.

(You may keep this handout.)

JOURNEY TO THE CROSS
Station 1
Outer Noise

Be still, and know that I am God! I will be honored by every nation. I will be honored throughout the world. —Psalm 46:10 (NLT)

This TV represents the noise and distractions of our lives.

Sometimes we're so caught up with the busyness of life that we tune out God. Even today as you came in, you have many thoughts going through your mind.

Take a moment to acknowledge the static in your mind.

Turn off the TV. Look at the blank screen. Use its stillness as a reminder to quiet your spirit before God.

Take a moment to be still and know that God *is God*.

Ask God to quiet your thoughts and put aside distractions so you can focus on God and hear God's voice through this journey.

Before you move to the next station, turn the TV back on for the next person.

(You may keep this handout.)

JOURNEY TO THE CROSS
Station 2
God in the Flesh

So the Word became human and made his home among us. He was full of unfailing love and faithfulness. And we have seen his glory, the glory of the Father's one and only Son. —John 1:14 (NLT)

Today you're invited on a journey through the last days and hours of Jesus' life.

In front of you is a pair of sandals, the kind that any ordinary person would wear.

As you begin this journey, focus on what it means for the eternal God to become a human. Think about what it means that Jesus once stood in sandals like these, just like any of us might do. God, who created the world, stepped into an ordinary human body.

Take time to meditate on the mystery, majesty, and humility of Jesus, the Son of God, and write down some of your thoughts.

(You may keep this handout.)

JOURNEY TO THE CROSS
Station 3
Mary Anoints Jesus

Six days before the Passover celebration began, Jesus arrived in Bethany, the home of Lazarus—the man he had raised from the dead. A dinner was prepared in Jesus' honor. Martha served, and Lazarus was among those who ate with him. Then Mary took a twelve-ounce jar of expensive perfume made from essence of nard, and she anointed Jesus' feet with it, wiping his feet with her hair. The house was filled with the fragrance.

But Judas Iscariot, the disciple who would soon betray him, said, "That perfume was worth a year's wages. It should have been sold and the money given to the poor." Not that he cared for the poor—he was a thief, and since he was in charge of the disciples' money, he often stole some for himself.

Jesus replied, "Leave her alone. She did this in preparation for my burial. You will always have the poor among you, but you will not always have me." —John 12:1-8 (NLT)

Mary poured out expensive perfume onto Jesus' feet as an act of worship. Place a drop or two of oil on a cotton ball. Smell its fragrance. The fragrance may not be strong at first, but you'll smell it for hours. It's long lasting.

Mary's act of worship was pure…passionate…real…expensive…extravagant. And it touched the heart of Jesus. Jesus knew he was headed to the cross, and Mary's act of worship was a blessing to him.

How can you pour out your love to Jesus extravagantly—in a way that will spread the beautiful fragrance of Jesus where you are?

When you leave, take the cotton ball with you. Let its fragrance remind you that we're called to live every moment of our lives in fragrant worship of Jesus.

(You may keep this handout.)

JOURNEY TO THE CROSS
Station 4
Judas Agrees to Betray Jesus

Then Judas Iscariot, one of the twelve disciples, went to the leading priests and asked, "How much will you pay me to betray Jesus to you?" And they gave him thirty pieces of silver. From that time on, Judas began looking for an opportunity to betray Jesus. —Matthew 26:14-16 (NLT)

Judas was one of Jesus' friends, one of the 12 disciples who'd been with him for three years. He agreed to betray Jesus for just 30 silver coins—the equivalent of about three months' pay.

Hold one or two of the coins in your hand. How could Judas betray Jesus, his friend, for money?

How do you think Judas felt when he looked at the coins in his hand and realized what he'd traded for them?

Is your own heart tempted to betray Jesus over material things?

(You may keep this handout.)

5 JOURNEY TO THE CROSS
Station 5
The Last Supper

Now Jesus was deeply troubled, and he exclaimed, "I tell you the truth, one of you will betray me!"

The disciples looked at each other, wondering whom he could mean. The disciple Jesus loved was sitting next to Jesus at the table. Simon Peter motioned to him to ask, "Who's he talking about?" So that disciple leaned over to Jesus and asked, "Lord, who is it?"

Jesus responded, "It is the one to whom I give the bread I dip in the bowl." And when he had dipped it, he gave it to Judas, son of Simon Iscariot. When Judas had eaten the bread, Satan entered into him. Then Jesus told him, "Hurry and do what you're going to do." None of the others at the table knew what Jesus meant. Since Judas was their treasurer, some thought Jesus was telling him to go and pay for the food or to give some money to the poor. So Judas left at once, going out into the night. —John 13:21-30 (NLT)

Jesus was celebrating the Passover feast with his disciples.

Tear off a piece of bread, dip it into the oil, and eat it as Jesus did. As you're eating, think of the heartbreak he must have been feeling after being betrayed by one of his own disciples. He knew his disciples would soon face confusion and fear.

Contemplate his sorrow and compassion for them.

(You may keep this handout.)

JOURNEY TO THE CROSS
Station 6
Gethsemane

Then Jesus went with them to the olive grove called Gethsemane, and he said, "Sit here while I go over there to pray." He took Peter and Zebedee's two sons, James and John, and he became anguished and distressed. He told them, "My soul is crushed with grief to the point of death. Stay here and keep watch with me."

He went on a little farther and bowed with his face to the ground, praying, "My Father! If it is possible, let this cup of suffering be taken away from me. Yet I want your will to be done, not mine."

Then he returned to the disciples and found them asleep. He said to Peter, "Couldn't you watch with me even one hour? Keep watch and pray, so that you will not give in to temptation. For the spirit is willing, but the body is weak!"

Then Jesus left them a second time and prayed, "My Father! If this cup cannot be taken away unless I drink it, your will be done." When he returned to them again, he found them sleeping, for they couldn't keep their eyes open.

So he went to pray a third time, saying the same things again. Then he came to the disciples and said, "Go ahead and sleep. Have your rest. But look—the time has come. The Son of Man is betrayed into the hands of sinners. Up, let's be going. Look, my betrayer is here!" —Matthew 26:36-46 (NLT)

This scene reveals the sorrow in Jesus' heart that night. He prayed to his Father that he wouldn't have to go to the cross if there were any other way. Yet Jesus prayed the hardest prayer any of us can pray: "Yet I want your will, not mine."

JOURNEY TO THE CROSS Station 6: Gethsemane

When Jesus said, "Let this cup of suffering be taken away from me," he was anticipating the time of tremendous pain that he would soon face.

Pour a cup of grape juice and drink it. As you do, remember that Jesus chose to bear the agony of the cross—to drink the cup—to save us.

Is there a cup that God is asking you to drink—something for which you need to pray the prayer of Gethsemane: "Yet I want your will, not mine"?

(You may keep this handout.)

7 JOURNEY TO THE CROSS
Station 7
Jesus' Arrest

After saying these things, Jesus crossed the Kidron Valley with his disciples and entered a grove of olive trees. Judas, the betrayer, knew this place, because Jesus had often gone there with his disciples. The leading priests and Pharisees had given Judas a contingent of Roman soldiers and Temple guards to accompany him. Now with blazing torches, lanterns, and weapons, they arrived at the olive grove.

Jesus fully realized all that was going to happen to him, so he stepped forward to meet them. "Who are you looking for?" he asked.

"Jesus the Nazarene," they replied.

"I AM he," Jesus said. (Judas, who betrayed him, was standing with them.) As Jesus said "I AM he," they all drew back and fell to the ground! Once more he asked them, "Who are you looking for?"

And again they replied, "Jesus the Nazarene."

"I told you that I AM he," Jesus said. "And since I am the one you want, let these others go." He did this to fulfill his own statement: "I did not lose a single one of those you have given me."

Then Simon Peter drew a sword and slashed off the right ear of Malchus, the high priest's slave. But Jesus said to Peter, "Put your sword back into its sheath. Shall I not drink from the cup of suffering the Father has given me?" —John 18:1-11 (NLT)

Even though Jesus could have fought the guards, he let himself be bound and led away.

Pick up the rope and hold it in your hands. Remember that Jesus was bound with a rope like this one.

He chose to submit to the difficult way of the cross with every step he took.

(You may keep this handout.)

8 JOURNEY TO THE CROSS
Station 8
Jesus' Trial

Those who had arrested Jesus took him to Caiaphas, the high priest, where the teachers of the law and the elders had assembled. But Peter followed at a distance, right up to the courtyard of the high priest. He entered and sat down with the guards to see the outcome.

The chief priests and the whole Sanhedrin were looking for false evidence against Jesus so that they could put him to death. But they did not find any, though many false witnesses came forward.

Then the governor's soldiers took Jesus into the Praetorium and gathered the whole company of soldiers around him. They stripped him and put a scarlet robe on him, and then twisted together a crown of thorns and set it on his head. They put a staff in his right hand and knelt in front of him and mocked him. "Hail, king of the Jews!" they said. They spit on him, and took the staff and struck him on the head again and again. After they had mocked him, they took off the robe and put his own clothes on him. Then they led him away to crucify him. —Matthew 26:57-60a; 27:27-31

Imagine yourself in Peter's shoes. You're looking out over the courtyard where Jesus is being tried and mocked. You know he's being unjustly accused.

As you stand here, you hear people telling lies about Jesus.

You watch him being beaten and mocked.

Here is the man you've followed for three years, the man you'd put all your hope in, being sentenced to death.

In your heart you've believed he is God, the promised Messiah of the Jewish people.

Your whole world is crashing around you, and—worst of all—you've denied that you even know him.

Look at the purple robe and the crown of thorns the angry soldiers used to wound and humiliate Jesus. What do you want to tell Jesus right now?

(You may keep this handout.)

9 JOURNEY TO THE CROSS
Station 9
Jesus' Crucifixion

As they were going out, they met a man from Cyrene, named Simon, and they forced him to carry the cross. They came to a place called Golgotha (which means "the place of the skull"). There they offered Jesus wine to drink, mixed with gall; but after tasting it, he refused to drink it. When they had crucified him, they divided up his clothes by casting lots. And sitting down, they kept watch over him there. Above his head they placed the written charge against him: THIS IS JESUS, THE KING OF THE JEWS.

Two rebels were crucified with him, one on his right and one on his left. Those who passed by hurled insults at him, shaking their heads and saying, "You who are going to destroy the temple and build it in three days, save yourself! Come down from the cross, if you are the Son of God!"

In the same way, the chief priests, the teachers of the law and the elders mocked him. "He saved others," they said, "but he can't save himself! He's the King of Israel! Let him come down now from the cross, and we will believe in him. He trusts in God. Let God rescue him now if he wants to, for he said, 'I am the Son of God.'"

In the same way the rebels who were crucified with him also heaped insults on him.
—Matthew 27:32-44

Here is Jesus dying a brutal death on a Roman cross—an instrument of torture.

Kneel in front of the cross. Imagine yourself at the scene. What's going through your mind? Don't rush through this part.

*HANDOUTS

Jesus' love for humans led him to the cross. He could have run away or fought or called angels to rescue him, but he didn't. He chose to stay.

Near you are several pieces of paper and some pens. Think of an area where you have rebelled, chosen your own way. It could be an attitude that you know in your heart is disappointing to God. Write it on a piece of paper. No one else will read it, but you can write it in code if you want to.

Then fold the paper in half. Pick up a hammer and a nail and nail it to the cross of Jesus. As you do, think about how Jesus' sacrifice was to empower you to live beyond all that which is keeping you from living God's ways.

With each strike of the hammer, remember Jesus' words: "It is finished."

(You may keep this handout.)

10 JOURNEY TO THE CROSS
Station 10
Jesus' Death

From noon until three in the afternoon darkness came over all the land. About three in the afternoon Jesus cried out in a loud voice, *"Eli, Eli, lema sabachthani?"* (which means, "My God, my God, why have you forsaken me?").

When some of those standing there heard this, they said, "He's calling Elijah."

Immediately one of them ran and got a sponge. He filled it with wine vinegar, put it on a staff, and offered it to Jesus to drink. The rest said, "Now leave him alone. Let's see if Elijah comes to save him."

And when Jesus had cried out again in a loud voice, he gave up his spirit.

At that moment the curtain of the temple was torn in two from top to bottom. The earth shook, the rocks split and the tombs broke open. The bodies of many holy people who had died were raised to life. They came out of the tombs after Jesus' resurrection and went into the holy city and appeared to many people.

When the centurion and those with him who were guarding Jesus saw the earthquake and all that had happened, they were terrified, and exclaimed, "Surely he was the Son of God!" —Matthew 27:45-54

When Jesus died, so many people watching must have thought their hopes had died, too.

Darkness came over all the land that day.

Choose a candle and extinguish it.

Remember the darkness that the whole world—and heaven itself—must have felt that day.

(You may keep this handout.)

JOURNEY TO THE CROSS
Station 11
Jesus' Burial

As evening approached, there came a rich man from Arimathea, named Joseph, who had himself become a disciple of Jesus. Going to Pilate, he asked for Jesus' body, and Pilate ordered that it be given to him. Joseph took the body, wrapped it in a clean linen cloth, and placed it in his own new tomb that he had cut out of the rock. He rolled a big stone in front of the entrance to the tomb and went away.

Mary Magdalene and the other Mary were sitting there opposite the tomb.
—Matthew 27:57-61

The rock you see here is just a fraction of the size of the rock that sealed Jesus' tomb.

Imagine the heaviness of it. Touch this rock. Feel its weight.

Can you sense the heavy weight the disciples, and those who loved Jesus, must have felt as Jesus' tomb was sealed? In their eyes, death had won.

This was a stone that no one could move. It was final. Jesus was gone and buried.

(You may keep this handout.)

JOURNEY TO THE CROSS
Station 12
Jesus' Resurrection

After the Sabbath, at dawn on the first day of the week, Mary Magdalene and the other Mary went to look at the tomb.

There was a violent earthquake, for an angel of the Lord came down from heaven and, going to the tomb, rolled back the stone and sat on it. His appearance was like lightning, and his clothes were white as snow. The guards were so afraid of him that they shook and became like dead men.

The angel said to the women, "Do not be afraid, for I know that you are looking for Jesus, who was crucified. He is not here; he has risen, just as he said. Come and see the place where he lay. Then go quickly and tell his disciples: 'He has risen from the dead and is going ahead of you into Galilee. There you will see him.' Now I have told you."

So the women hurried away from the tomb, afraid yet filled with joy, and ran to tell his disciples. Suddenly Jesus met them. "Greetings," he said. They came to him, clasped his feet and worshiped him. Then Jesus said to them, "Do not be afraid. Go and tell my brothers to go to Galilee; there they will see me." —Matthew 28:1-10

Imagine the cold and heavy fear and sorrow these women must have felt as they journeyed to the tomb that day. Imagine them arriving at the tomb and finding the stone rolled away, the empty grave clothes in the place where Jesus' body was supposed to be.

Imagine the shock and the overwhelming joy they felt as they met the risen Jesus in the garden.

Their Lord was alive! Imagine how these women were transformed in that moment.

How do you think the risen Jesus wants to transform you today?

(You may keep this handout.)

*HANDOUTS

13 JOURNEY TO THE CROSS
Station 13
Crossroads

Then Jesus said to his disciples, "Whoever wants to be my disciple must deny themselves and take up their cross and follow me." —Matthew 16:24

You've experienced some of the emotions that Jesus, the Son of God, experienced for you. You experienced the agony of surrender and obedience that Jesus Christ experienced.

Think about the journey you've just taken through the final days of Jesus' life, death, and beyond. His was no accidental journey. Every step Jesus took was purposeful, deliberate, by plan. Jesus bore every moment of pain, betrayal, and agony out of love for you. You were—and still are—a part of Christ's journey.

What will you do with Jesus?

You can, in your heart, choose to hold on to your own ways, take your own journey, and live life in your own strength.

Or you can leave clinging to the extravagant love and forgiveness of the One who died for you.

You can pursue Jesus, the God who pursued you all the way to the cross.

Will you choose to join with Jesus and live a different kind of life…a life of love and sacrifice?

It's your choice. You choose by praying the prayer of Gethsemane:

"Yet I want your will, not mine."

Spend a few quiet moments with Jesus now.

Write a prayer expressing your desire to surrender to Jesus and follow his way of life.

(You may keep this handout.)

RESTORATION

DEVELOPED BY MICHAEL NOVELLI
WITH KELLY DOLAN & MARK NOVELLI

*INSTRUCTIONS

DESCRIPTION

The Restoration Experience is designed to help participants think more deeply about how God is restoring them and how they're to be agents of restoration in the world.

LOCATIONS AND LOGISTICS

This experience does require a lot of planning ahead of time. Although it's only four stations, they take quite a bit of time to complete. It could easily be done outdoors.

GROUP SIZE

This can be done with a group of up to 40 people. That being said, it will probably work best with smaller groups of 20 or fewer, otherwise it may be hard to hear one another during the discussion.

STATIONS (STOPPING POINTS)

STATION 1: THE CONTINUING STORY
LOCATION AND PREPARATION

This station might work best indoors. Participants will do a creative retelling and act out seven episodes in God's Story. Divide everyone into groups of four to eight people. Assign each group one to two episodes in God's Story. Each group will need to pick a narrator who will read the story (narrative available on accompanying CD), and everyone else will play characters in the story. Participation is required! The characters don't need to say anything, just react as events happen in the story. In fact, they can even be objects—the wind, trees, whatever. Just be creative. Use sound effects, objects, drawings, costumes, and so on. The narrator should give the actors cues, stopping after key events or dialogue to allow the actors to respond. Have fun with this. It may help the groups if you provide a bunch of props—a trunk full of clothes or costumes, paper and scissors, and so on.

MATERIALS

- Echo's Seven Episodes handout—one copy for every three participants (available on accompanying CD).

- Copies of the Station 1 handouts for every participant (available on accompanying CD).

- Pens.

- A variety of items for storytelling props—a trunk full of clothes or costumes, paper and scissors, and so on.

STATION 2: RESTORATIVE COMMUNITY
LOCATION AND PREPARATION

Participants will consider what it means to be a community that's loving and restorative. They'll do some prayer activities involving various body positions—sitting in a circle, kneeling, and so on—so provide a large open space for this. This station would work great outdoors.

MATERIALS

- Copies of the Station 2 handouts for every participant (available on accompanying CD).

- Pens.

STATION 3: A LIVING MOSAIC

LOCATION AND PREPARATION

Participants will create a mosaic in the shape of a cross as they consider what it means to be part of the body of Christ. Pictures of ones I've created are available on accompanying CD. This station could work well indoors or outdoors.

MATERIALS

- Copies of the Station 3 handouts for every participant (available on accompanying CD).

- Pens.

- A mosaic—created in one of two ways.

Complex (for a group of 24 people or less—scale as needed)

- 16 x 20 inch piece of MDF board or Plexiglas, primed and painted.

- A cheap 16 x 20 inch frame (perhaps from a thrift store) with the glass removed.

- Multi-mastic tile adhesive—24-hour dry time.

- 24 two-inch square white bathroom tiles. (It's good to have a few extras, as some participants will want to create more than one tile.)

- Rocks or broken tiles to fill in around the cross.

Simple

- Cut 4" x 4" paper squares in a variety of colors—use cardstock if affixing it to a wall and regular paper if you're affixing it to a window. (Note: When it's affixed to a window, it will look like stained glass during the day.)

- Plan out how many you'll need to make a cross on the wall of your meeting room—24 is a good number.

- Double-sided or blue painter's tape to affix the squares to the wall.

STATION 4: BRINGING RESTORATION TO THE WORLD

LOCATION AND PREPARATION

Participants will brainstorm ways they can be agents of restoration each day. Participants will write ideas on Post-its and affix them to posters or a bulletin board with designated areas for home, school, neighborhood/city, and world.

MATERIALS

- Copies of the Station 4 handouts for every participant (available on accompanying CD).

- Posters or a bulletin board with designated areas for home, school, neighborhood/city, and world.

- Post-its—several for each participant.

- Pens.

ADDITIONAL ACTIVITY

ADULT READS (not in handouts):
We're connected to this story...called to live in the ways of the kingdom. This story is what identifies us and shapes us as people and as a community. To symbolize this, dip your thumb in the ink provided and make a thumbprint on the paper. And as you do this, thank God out loud for making you a part of his kingdom of restoration.

MATERIALS

- A table with one large piece of poster board or foam core board—large enough for each participant's fingerprint.

- Inkpads in a variety of colors.

- Wet wipes to clean ink off fingers.

- Trash can for used wet wipes.

RESTORATION
Introduction

EVERYONE READ SILENTLY

This is an important time to…

- Connect with God and
- Connect with others in meaningful ways.

This time requires you to…

- Slow down and turn off your cell phone.
- Enter into a different pace of life.
- Speak quietly and act respectfully.
- Think deeply and engage your mind and heart.
- Be open to what God has for you.

We hope that through this experience you'll see how your story is connected to and a continuation of a bigger Story that began thousands of years ago.

Pray quietly and ask God to help you enter the story.

You will enter this experience with your entire group. At each station, different people from your group will read parts aloud. You don't have to read if you don't want to, but as many people as possible should read and help guide the experience.

(You may keep this handout.)

*HANDOUTS

RESTORATION
Station 1
The Continuing Story

READER 1:

Everyone loves a good story.

How many times has a movie, a book, or a song made you feel something? Something deep and meaningful? Maybe something you couldn't even describe?

Stories have the power to take us on a journey. They show us new places and introduce us to new people. They draw us in…and we become a part of their adventure.

The best stories are the ones that show us something about ourselves. They unveil more of who we are—and who we could become.

READER 2:

God's Story is like this. It's a story full of mystery, action, miracles, war, drama, and love. It tells of a great and faithful Creator who reveals the best way to live a life of love, peace, and sacrifice. It stretches from the beginning of time, across our lives, and into the future.

It begins with new life emerging…

"In the beginning God created the heavens and the earth." —Genesis 1:1

And moves to completion with new life emerging again…

"I am making everything new!" —Revelation 21:5

READER 3:

God, the great Author, continues to write this Story and desires us to find ourselves in it, discovering who we are and why we're here.

Are you starting to see it? Are you catching a glimpse of how this amazing Story is your story?

RESTORATION Station 1: The Continuing Story

Let's take a look at this amazing Story in a different way…

Split up into groups of four to eight people.

READER 4:

All of the groups will be assigned one to two episodes in God's Story. Each group will need to choose a narrator who will read the story *(narrative provided)*, and everyone else will play characters in the story. Participation is required.

The characters don't need to say anything but just react as events happen in the story. In fact, you can be objects—the wind, trees, whatever. BE CREATIVE! Use sound effects, objects, drawings, costumes, and so on. You can use whatever you find in the room as a prop.

The narrator should give cues, stopping after key events or dialogue to allow the actors to respond. Have fun with this.

In 15 minutes the groups will present their episodes for the group to enjoy.

Give the groups the Seven Episodes handouts from Echo.

DISCUSS (AFTER YOUR STORY PRESENTATIONS)

*   As you read or listened to this narrative, what did you picture in your mind?
*   What does each story show us about God's kingdom ways?
*   What do you think God's Story is ultimately about?
*   How does this story continue right now? How are we a part of it?

READER 5:

We're a part of this continuing story, called to live in the ways of the kingdom. God desires to restore humans to reflect God's image perfectly—as we once did in the garden. This story is what identifies us and shapes us as individuals and as a community.

*HANDOUTS

READER 1:

I will read the epilogue to this story again:

> The end of this amazing story lies ahead…

> Jesus promised to come back one day, saying, "When I return again, everyone will know I am here. It'll be like a huge flash of lightning that fills the sky!"

> Jesus will return to destroy all evil, sin, and rebellion. There will be no more sickness, pain, or death. He will wipe away every tear from our eyes. The world as we know it will be gone forever. Humans will receive new bodies and live on a new earth, restored back to the way God designed it. God's kingdom will come in fullness, and everything will live under God's rule.

> As God's community on earth, we wait with great anticipation for this amazing day. Until then, may we live in God's ways, giving people a glimpse of what life is like in the coming kingdom of God.

EVERYONE PRAY

> God,
>
> Thank you for giving us this wonderful story.
>
> May we find ourselves in it and allow it to shape our lives.
>
> Help us join in your mission of love and restoration each day.
>
> Amen.

Proceed to the next station.

(You may keep this handout.)

RESTORATION
Station 2
Restorative Community

READER 1:

To restore something is to return it to its intended design—to make it new again. That's exactly what God is doing with us—repairing, healing, reorienting us toward the wholeness we were created with.

"I am making everything new!" —Revelation 21:5

We're like shattered mirrors. We're still reflecting—in part—the beautiful nature of God that's within us, but the image is distorted by our selfishness and fear. God is taking the broken pieces of our lives and putting them back together and shaping us back into wholeness.

READER 2:

I will give you a new heart and put a new spirit in you; I will remove from you your heart of stone and give you a heart of flesh. And I will put my Spirit in you and move you to follow my decrees and be careful to keep my laws. —Ezekiel 36:26-27

Slowly God's image comes into focus as we allow the Spirit to work in and through us, and the beauty and uniqueness that God created in us shines through.

Take a minute and thank God for already bringing restoration in your life. Ask God to bring healing and hope to areas in which you're hurting and afraid.

READER 3:

The restoration that is happening inside of us is also supposed to happen through us. We're being made new so we can help bring hope, healing, and justice to others.

Therefore, if anyone is in Christ, the new creation has come: The old has gone, the new is here! All this is from God, who reconciled us to himself through Christ and gave us the ministry of reconciliation: that God was reconciling the world to himself in Christ,

not counting people's sins against them. And he has committed to us the message of reconciliation. We are therefore Christ's ambassadors, as though God were making his appeal through us. We implore you on Christ's behalf: Be reconciled to God. —2 Corinthians 5:17-20

READER 4:

We can't do this alone…we must rely on the Holy Spirit to empower us to follow in the ways of Jesus. We must also rely on each other, surrounding ourselves with a community of believers to support and challenge us toward continuing on.

> Your love for one another will prove to the world that you are my disciples. —John 13:35 (NLT)

> Let's see how inventive we can be in encouraging love and helping out, not avoiding worshiping together as some do but spurring each other on. —Hebrews 10:22-25 (*The Message*)

READER 5:

Let's look at how the first church lived, as described in the book of Acts…

> All the believers devoted themselves to the apostles' teaching, and to fellowship, and to sharing in meals (including the Lord's Supper), and to prayer. A deep sense of awe came over them all, and the apostles performed many miraculous signs and wonders. And all the believers met together in one place and shared everything they had. They sold their property and possessions and shared the money with those in need. They worshiped together at the Temple each day, met in homes for the Lord's Supper, and shared their meals with great joy and generosity—all the while praising God and enjoying the goodwill of all the people. And each day the Lord added to their fellowship those who were being saved. —Acts 2:42-47 (NLT)

The people in the first church experienced God's community in such amazing ways that they reordered their entire lives around it. This is the kind of community we're called to create—a distinct

group of people who will show the world what it means to live in God's ways and extend his blessing to the entire world—a community of restoration, healing, and hope.

EVERYONE PRAY

1. Put your **hands over your hearts** and quietly pray that God's love will continue to deepen in your hearts, restoring you to wholeness.

2. Get in a circle and put your **arms on the shoulders** of the people standing next to you *(like a football huddle)*. Take turns praying out loud that God will grow your group closer together and that you'll live in unity with one another. *(This is also a great time to confess ways in which you haven't been loving, serving, and including each other.)*

3. Get down on your **knees.** As people reflecting God's kingdom, we're to be servants of all. Take turns praying now that you'd seek to serve those in your group.

4. Still in a close circle, **face outward** with your palms open. This posture is to remind us that we're to bring God's restoration to all we meet. Take turns praying for your friends and family who need God's touch.

Proceed to the next station.

(You may keep this handout.)

RESTORATION
Station 3
A Living Mosaic

READER 1:

We, as followers of Christ, are part of something bigger than ourselves. We're the continuation of God's Story as the "body of Christ," led by the Holy Spirit to be the physical presence of Jesus in our world.

> Now you are the body of Christ, and each one of you is a part of it. —1 Corinthians 12:27

READER 2:

> A mosaic consists of thousands of little stones. Some are blue, some are green, some are yellow, some are gold. When we bring our faces close to the mosaic, we can admire the beauty of each stone. But as we step back from it, we can see that all these little stones reveal to us a beautiful picture, telling a story none of these stones can tell by itself.

> That is what our life in community is about. Each of us is like a little stone, but together we reveal the face of God to the world. Nobody can say: "I make God visible." But others who see us together can say: "They make God visible." Community is where humility and glory touch." —Henri Nouwen[22]

CREATING OUR MOSAIC

Each of you received a tile. This tile represents you and your part in God's kingdom. Use markers to make this tile uniquely yours. Do this as an act of prayer that describes your love for God. Put your initials on the tile.

> After you're finished, bring it over to the mosaic and we'll affix it with the rest of the group's tiles.

READER 3:

In a real way, Jesus is still here in the flesh. But now, instead of looking at the world through one pair of eyes, he sees through millions. Instead of touching and smiling and crying and laughing and welcoming and listening through two eyes, hands, and ears, Jesus does so through one body composed of millions of us!

EVERYONE READ OUT LOUD (SLOWLY, TWICE)

"Christ has no body but yours,

No hands, no feet on earth but yours,

Yours are the eyes through which he looks

Compassion on this world,

Yours are the feet with which he walks to do good,

Yours are the hands, with which he blesses all the world.

Yours are the hands, yours are the feet,

Yours are the eyes, you are his body.

Christ has no body now but yours." Amen.

(Quote from St. Teresa of Avila)

Proceed to the last station.

(You may keep this handout.)

*HANDOUTS

4

RESTORATION
Station 4
Bringing Restoration to the World

READER 1:

Let's take a look at what Jesus says a life of bringing kingdom restoration might look like:

> Go to the lost, confused people right here in the neighborhood. Tell them that the kingdom is here. Bring health to the sick. Raise the dead. Touch the untouchables. Kick out the demons. You have been treated generously, so live generously.

> Don't think you have to put on a fund-raising campaign before you start. You don't need a lot of equipment. You are the equipment, and all you need to keep that going is three meals a day. Travel light.

> Stay alert. This is hazardous work I'm assigning you. You're going to be like sheep running through a wolf pack, so don't call attention to yourselves. Be as cunning as a snake, inoffensive as a dove.

READER 2:

> Don't be naive. Some people will impugn your motives; others will smear your reputation—just because you believe in me. Don't be upset when they haul you before the civil authorities. Without knowing it, they've done you—and me—a favor; they've given you a platform for preaching the kingdom news! And don't worry about what you'll say or how you'll say it. The right words will be there; the Spirit of your Father will supply the words.

> When people realize it is the living God you are presenting and not some idol that makes them feel good, they are going to turn on you, even people in your own family. There is a great irony here: Proclaiming so much love, experiencing so much hate. But don't quit. Don't cave in. It is all well worth it in the end.

> This is a large work I've called you into, but don't be overwhelmed by it. It's best to start small. Give a cool cup of water to someone who is thirsty, for instance. The smallest act of giving or receiving makes you a true apprentice. You won't lose out on a thing. —Jesus (Matthew 10:5-8, 9-10, 16, 17-20, 21-23, 41-42, *The Message*)

RESTORATION Station 4: Bringing Restoration to the World

Now take a moment and read through these verses again on your own.

DISCUSS (IN GROUPS OF THREE)

- What images or phrases stood out to you from these verses?
- Is this the kind of life you picture when you think of following God? Why or why not?
- Is this the kind of life you'd pictured for yourself?
- Based on these verses, what do you think it looks like to live out God's kingdom? Share your answer to this last question with the other groups.

BRAINSTORM

Take a few minutes to write or draw a prayer on the posters. They're divided into the following categories: Home, school, neighborhood/city, and world.

Think about:

- How is God calling you to make a difference?
- What dreams is God putting in your heart and mind?
- How can your church and youth group join in with you?

Take a moment on your own and think of some specific people you see at home and at school. Come up with some ways you can bring God's kingdom of love and restoration to them. Write your ideas on sticky notes and put them on the posters.

After a few minutes, continue…

As a whole group, come up with specific ways you can bring God's kingdom of love and restoration to your city and world. DREAM BIG! As you come up with an idea, share it with your group and then write it on a Post-it and attach it to the posters under the appropriate category.

(You may keep this handout.)

LIST OF CD RESOURCES

1. Creation

- Handouts for each station
- Supply list and logistics page
- Leaf shape outlines handout (Stations 3 and 4)
- Example images

2. Disruption

- Handouts for each station
- Supply list and logistics page
- List of recommended images to purchase from iStock Photo
- Example images

3. Israel's Journey

- Handouts for each station
- Supply list and logistics page
- Example images

4. The Tabernacle

- Handouts for each station
- Supply list and logistics page
- Example images
- Information on where to purchase an image of the Tabernacle

5. The Kingdom

- Handouts for each station
- Supply list and logistics page
- Situation Puzzle handout
- The Forgotten picture backgrounds
- List of recommended Kingdom images to purchase from iStock Photo
- Pictures of the forgotten
- Pretzel-Making Instructions handout
- Parable Pictures backgrounds
- List of recommended Parable images to purchase from iStock Photo
- Example images

6. Journey to the Cross

- Handouts for each station
- Supply list and logistics page
- Example images

7. Restoration

- Handouts for each station
- Echo's Seven Episodes handout
- Supply list and logistics page
- Example images

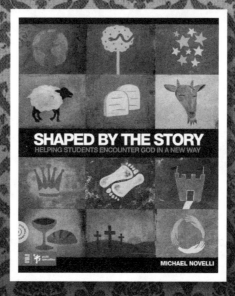

Through the art of "Storying," your students will experience God in a new way. This unique, dialogue-centered approach will spark imaginations and inspire your group to find themselves in God's amazing story.

Shaped by the Story
Helping Students Encounter God in a New Way

Michael Novelli
Retail $29.99
978-0-310-27366-0

Visit www.youthspecialties.com
or your local bookstore.